D0431668

TEACHING
ACTS

Unlocking the book of Acts for the Bible Teacher

DAVID COOK

SERIES EDITORS: DAVID JACKMAN & ROBIN SYDSERFF

For Elisa, Joanna, Ashleigh, Ben and Luke.

'Like arrows in the hands of a warrior'

TEACHING
ACTS

Unlocking the book of Acts for the Bible Teacher

DAVID COOK

SERIES EDITORS: DAVID JACKMAN & ROBIN SYDSERFF

PTMEDIA

CHRISTIAN
FOCUS

Unless otherwise indicated all Scripture quotations are taken from the Holy Bible, New International Version. Copyright © 1973, 1978, 1984 by International Bible Society. Used by permission of Hodder & Stoughton Publishers, A member of the Hodder Headline Group. All rights reserved. 'NIV' is a registered trademark of International Bible Society. UK trademark number 1448790.

Scripture quotations marked ESV are taken from *The Holy Bible, English Standard Version*. Copyright © 2001 by Crossway Bibles, a publishing ministry of Good News Publishers. Used by permission. All rights reserved.

Copyright © Proclamation Trust Media 2007

ISBN 978-1-84550-255-3

10 9 8 7 6 5 4 3 2 1

Published in 2007,
reprinted 2008, 2012 and 2014
by
Christian Focus Publications Ltd.,
Geanies House, Fearn,
Ross-shire, IV20 1TW, Scotland, Great Britain
with
Proclamation Trust Media,
Willcox House, 140-148 Borough High Street,
London, SE1 1LB, England, Great Britain.
www.proctrust.org.uk

www.christianfocus.com

Cover design by Moose77.com
Printed and bound by Norhaven, Denmark

All rights reserved. No part of this publication may be reproduced, stored in a retrieval system, or transmitted, in any form, by any means, electronic, mechanical, photocopying, recording or otherwise without the prior permission of the publisher or a license permitting restricted copying. In the U.K. such licenses are issued by the Copyright Licensing Agency, Saffron House, 6-10 Kirby Street, London, EC1 8TS www.cla.co.uk.

Contents

SERIES PREFACE

Whether you are a preacher, a small group Bible study leader or a youth worker, the *Teach the Bible* series will be an ideal companion in your study. Few commentaries are written specifically with the preacher or Bible teacher in mind, and with the sermon or Bible study as the point of reference. The preacher or teacher, the sermon or talk, and the listener are the key 'drivers' in this series.

The books are purposely practical, seeking to offer real help for those involved in teaching the Bible to others. The opening chapter offers an overview of the book (*Getting Our Bearings in Acts*), identifying key themes, structure, literary style etc. Chapter 2 suggests how the material might best be divided up for preaching or teaching (*Planning A Series on Acts*). This outline provides the framework for the meat of the book, with a separate chapter devoted to each sermon / Bible study. The content of these chapters is neither commentary nor sermon, but specifically geared to help the teacher get to grips with the text with its intended purpose clearly in view, its proclamation as the living Word of God. Chapters follow a consistent structure: 'Listening to the Text', 'From Text to Teaching' and 'Proclaiming the Message' (which includes a suggested preaching outline and format for a Bible study).

We are delighted that David Cook has written *Teaching Acts* for the series. Acts is a tough book to teach, but vital for the Church in every generation. David's wealth of experience in teaching Acts to generations of students at Sydney Missionary and Bible College is evident in the careful and logical way he unlocks the text. Above all, he is a passionate preacher and the best books for preachers are invariably written by preachers! We trust that *Teaching Acts* will be a welcome companion at your desk, helping you to arm the Spirit with His sword, as you participate in God's mission to the ends of the earth.

Our thanks to Tim McMahon, Moira Anderson, Zoe Harris and Anne Sydserff for editorial assistance and, as ever, to the team at Christian Focus for their committed partnership in this project.

David Jackman and Robin Sydserff,
Series Editors, London, January 2007

Author's Preface

This book is written for preachers. Preachers are busy people. As well as preparing to preach with some expertise at least once each Sunday, they generally have to administrate, coordinate, chair, visit, console, counsel, rebuke, correct and evangelize! For this reason, books for preachers, such as those in this series, must strive to be succinct.

The introductory chapters will help preachers get their bearings in Acts, and then to prepare three teaching series to take a congregation or small group through the whole book of Acts. Each of the main chapters takes the preacher through the process of preparing an expository sermon from the text. They include comments on the text and its context, identification of the big idea and the big questions raised by the text which the sermon will seek to answer, some possible points of contact between the message and the audience, dominant pictures which engage the hearer, and some hints on the application of the passage. Issues of application are always difficult, however. In an interview for the *Leadership Journal*, Haddon Robinson comments that 'more heresy is preached in application than in Bible exegesis' ("The Heresy of Application", *Leadership Journal*, Oct 1, 1997). Readers are referred to the book, *How to Prepare a Bible Talk*, published by SMBC Press (2003) and my chapters, "A Method of Preparation" and "Illustration and Application", for an elaboration of the need for Big Idea, Big Question, Dominant Picture and Application in expository preaching.

A word of warning! Too often as preachers we let the commentaries do our thinking for us. Under pressure, we immediately go to the commentaries, without first thoughtfully reading the text itself. If that is our 'method', our preaching is likely to be a regurgitation of the commentator's thoughts on a passage. The result is powerless preaching. Read the text thoroughly and thoughtfully, using different translations, and only then consult the commentaries for extra insights, clarification etc. So if you haven't done so already, start reading the text of Acts!

I am grateful to the faculty and students of Sydney Missionary and Bible College who listened and gave feedback on a series of sermons on Acts, delivered in Principal's Hour in 2006. Thank you to Kay Hoe Tan for his research assistance and to Tim McMahon who edited the manuscript. Tim's attention to detail and ability to turn preached material into written form were invaluable. Finally, thank you to all the team at The Proclamation Trust, particularly Robin Sydserff, for his enthusiastic commitment to this series.

I trust that you find this book a help as you seek to be a faithful and engaging preacher of the book of Acts.

David Cook,
Sydney, December 2006

I

GETTING OUR BEARINGS IN ACTS

The receiving society in the time of Acts

The great diversity of the society to which the gospel came in the first century AD is in many ways much like the multicultural society of today. Christianity in the time of Acts was one among many religions. As well as the dominant religion of Judaism there were followers of the Greek gods – Artemis (19:27-28, 35), Zeus (14:12-13) and Hermes (14:12). There were many religious figures – sorcerers (13:8ff), fortune tellers (16:16) and Jewish exorcists such as the Sons of Sceva (19:14) and Elymas (13:8). The language groups in Acts 2 evidence the diversity of cultures, even in Jerusalem. An individual had the ability and opportunity to pick and choose regarding their belief. Within Judaism, Pharisees believed in the resurrection of the dead, while Sadducees, the Bible-carrying clerics, did not. Then there were the philosophical schools of the Greeks: the Stoics who pursued knowledge and a virtuous life in apathy, and the Epicureans who sought after happiness in serene detachment. Both are mentioned in Acts 17:18.

Over all this diversity was the Roman insistence on tolerance. For Rome, religion was not about conviction, but superstitious ritual which did not affect everyday life at any profound level. 'Nike' was the religion of Rome: 'just do it', offer your sacrifices, go your way, live your life, don't give the gods a second thought, for they are not concerned about you! That's why many Romans found the Jews fascinating. Their religion affected their lives - the way they worked, rested, ate, etc. - in stark contrast to the Roman conception of religion.

In an environment of such diversity, the Roman Empire was uncompromising in its commitment to maintain unity. This was done by requiring all citizens to sacrifice to the gods (which included the Emperor) regardless of their other religious beliefs. All religions were tolerated as long as they tolerated other religions, including the Emperor cult.

Tolerance was the great civil imperative, but Christians knew that it was a spiritual impossibility because of the unique claims of the Lord Jesus. The way the apostles confronted this culture provides a model for the church today. The church made every attempt to communicate sensitively without being offensive (see the way they preached in synagogues, market places and fields in 4:19-20; 13:16-41; 14:15-17; 17:30-31). However, eternal salvation was at stake and Christians had a jealous regard for God's honour, so they were clear and could not be silenced. They determinedly sought to communicate the gospel faithfully in all the diverse situations that confronted them. Note Peter's twin convictions in 5:29, 32 – the apostles were the *commissioned witnesses of God* and *co-witnesses with God's Spirit* of the life, death and resurrection of Jesus Christ. The gospel, focusing on Jesus, was therefore preached fearlessly in country, city, synagogue, market place, and field; and hearers were called upon to repent and trust in Jesus Christ (Acts 20:21).

The author

Luke is not explicitly attributed with the authorship of Acts in the text of the book itself. However, authorship has been consistently attributed to Luke from the latter part of the second century (for example, by Irenaeus in the *Anti-Marcionite Prologue* and *Muratorian Canon*). But the strongest reason for accepting Luke's authorship comes from a comparison of the texts of Luke and Acts. Acts evidences an author whose writing style and interests match those of the author of the Gospel of Luke. Both have a great interest in:

+ **the ministry of the Spirit** (cf. Luke 1:35, 41, 67; 2:25; 3:16, 22; 4:1; 11:13; 12:12; 24:49; Acts 1:2, 16; 2:4, 33; 4:8; 10:44; 16:6);
+ **prayer** (Luke 1:10, 13; 2:37; 5:16; 6:12, 28; 11:1ff, 18:1-8; 19:46; 21:36; 22:39-46; Acts 1:14, 24-25; 2:42; 3:1; 4:24-30; 6:4, 6:1; 7:59-60; 8:14-24; 9:40; 10:2; 14:23; 28:8);
+ **God's interest in outcasts** (cf. Luke 4:18, 25-27; 5:29-30; 7:11-12, 22, 31-32, 37-50; 8:2-3; 13:11; 16:19-31; 19:1ff; Acts 5:12-16; 6; 8:4-8; 9:32ff; 12:12-17; 16:12-15; 18:24ff);
+ **the fact that the gospel is for the world** (Luke 2:10, 32; 3:4-6; 10:30-37; 13:29; 17:16; 19:10; 24:46-47;

Acts 1:8; 2:17-21; 5:32; 9:15; 10:35, 45; 11:18; 13:39, 47; 14:1; 15; 17:24-31; 22:15-16, 21; 28:28).

There is a close similarity between the introductions of Luke and Acts (Luke 1:1-4; Acts 1:1-2). In the introduction of Acts, the author refers to his 'former book' and both volumes are dedicated to Theophilus (Luke 1:3; Acts 1:1).

The author of Acts refers to himself as a companion of Paul, locating himself in the narrative with 'we' references (16:10-17; 20:5-15; 21:1-18; 27:1-28:16). Colossians 4:7-14 and Philemon 23-24 tell us who Paul's companions were during his imprisonment in Rome. In Colossians 4:14, Luke is referred to as 'dear friend' and 'doctor', suggesting that he was a long-term companion of Paul.

Similar introductions, style, interests, and the fact that the Acts narrative begins where the Gospel narrative concludes, all point to Acts as Volume 2 of Luke's work. In Volume 1 we find a record of 'all that Jesus began to do and teach' (Acts 1:1). In Acts we find the church proclaiming the salvation which is found in Christ. It records the continuation of the ministry of the now ascended Christ through his Holy Spirit, who brings people to the experience of salvation through hearing the gospel.

Acts as historical narrative

The book of Acts, like many Old Testament books such as Judges, Samuel, Kings and Chronicles, is an example of historical narrative. Though common in the Old Testament, Acts is the only pure example of this literary genre in the New Testament. Of course, the Gospels are narrative accounts of the life, death and resurrection of the Lord Jesus, but they are not typical narrative. In the Gospels,

Jesus adds his authoritative, interpretive word to explain the events recorded.

In Acts, the narrator, Luke, is far less prominent. He leaves clues as to what he believes to be important, he passes comment, but he does so in far more subtle ways than by using the direct interpretive word.

In the history of the interpretation of Acts, some scholars have focused on Luke's sources, some have questioned the historicity of Acts and others have spent a good deal of time defending his historical integrity. There is a tendency to read Luke in the light of Paul and use Acts merely as background for Paul's letters. But in the New Testament, Luke has written as much as Paul, so it is good for us to be thinking specifically about Luke and his interests, and not just see him as a foil for Paul. F. Scott Spencer's, *A Literary-Cultural Reading of Acts*, is refreshing. He accepts the text of Acts in its final form as Luke's work, and draws conclusions about what is important to Luke from a close examination of the text itself, without paying undue attention to source and context. Similarly, Tannehill comments: 'I do not explore the possible sources of Acts and seldom comment on the historical events that may lie behind the story, for these interests would lead me away from my main concern with the significance of the narrative in its finished form. Past concern with sources and historical events has sometimes led to hypotheses that stretched beyond the available evidence' (Tannehill, *The Narrative Unity of Luke and Acts*, 1990, p. 4).

Structure and chronology

Luke aims to provide an *orderly* account for Theophilus, consistent with his stated purpose in Volume 1 (Luke 1:3).

In Acts 1:8 he reveals the structure that will shape the whole book: '... you will receive power when the Holy Spirit comes on you; and you will be witnesses in Jerusalem, and in all Judea and Samaria, and to the ends of the earth'. The narrative centres on Jerusalem and Judea in chapters 1-7; on Samaria in the transitional period (ch. 8-12); and then finally on the Gentile world, beginning in Asia and Europe, and ending up in Rome (ch. 13-28).

TABLE 1: THE NARRATIVE STRUCTURE OF ACTS

Ref.	Region	Dominant Apostle	Evangelistic Target	Gentile focus
Ch. 1-7	Jerusalem and Judea	Peter	Jews	Ethiopian eunuch converted
Ch. 8-12	Samaria	Peter	Jews Samaritans God-fearers	Saul converted and commissioned as apostle to the Gentiles
Ch. 13-28	Gentile territory (Rome the destination)	Paul	Gentiles (but Jews first)	Antioch the sending church

In terms of chronology, my best efforts have come up with the following dates. There is a great deal of debate in the commentaries about these dates, but this may serve as a helpful general guide.

TABLE 2: THE CHRONOLOGY OF ACTS

A.D.	Event in Acts	Ref.
c. 33	Pentecost	2:1-11
33-34	Stephen's murder > dispersion Paul's conversion and commissioning Paul's period in Arabia	8:1 9:1-19 Gal. 1:17
35	Paul's first post-conversion visit to Jerusalem Antioch church established	9:26-28 11:19-21
43/44	James executed	12:1-2
46/47	Paul's second visit to Jerusalem	11:27-30
48	First missionary journey	Ch. 13-14
49	Council of Jerusalem	15:1-35
49-52	Second missionary journey (Paul in Corinth 50-52)	15:36-18:22
52-57	Third missionary journey (Paul in Ephesus 52-55)	18:23-20:38
57	Paul visits Jerusalem	Ch. 21-23

57-59	Paul imprisoned in Caesarea	Ch. 24-26
59-60	Paul's voyage to Rome	Ch. 27-28
65	Death of Paul in Rome	

Narrative flow

When preaching on narrative it is important to have an eye for movements. Normally, narrative preaching involves preaching on larger sections of text, so the ability to summarise is especially important. In many ways, the art of preaching is the art of summary.

In order to summarise a narrative, the preacher needs to isolate the steps in the development of the narrative and find the links between the steps. I find it helpful to draw up networking diagrams. The following diagrams serve as useful reference points for plotting your way through the book and, in particular, mapping the geographical spread of the gospel from Jerusalem and Judea, to Samaria, into

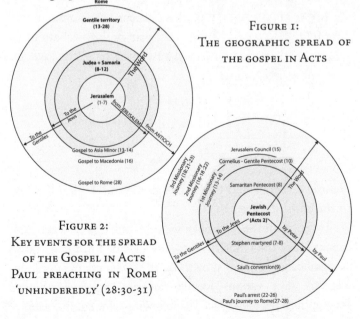

FIGURE 1:
THE GEOGRAPHIC SPREAD OF
THE GOSPEL IN ACTS

FIGURE 2:
KEY EVENTS FOR THE SPREAD
OF THE GOSPEL IN ACTS
PAUL PREACHING IN ROME
'UNHINDEREDLY' (28:30-31)

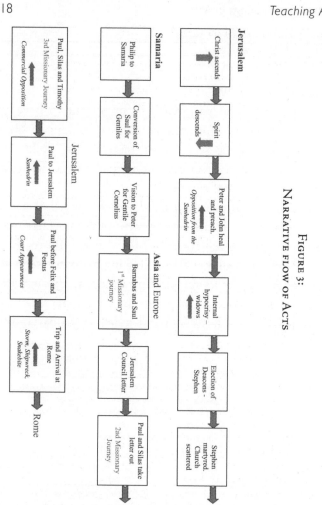

FIGURE 3:
NARRATIVE FLOW OF ACTS

Gentile territory, and finally to Rome (and, by implication, to the ends of the earth).

Throughout the text, Luke includes markers indicating the expansion of the Church. These are included in the narrative at significant points of growth or at key points of transition. Markers take various forms: statistics, repeated phrases, geographical references etc. The following table summarises.

TABLE 3: KEY GROWTH MARKERS

Ref.	Event in Acts
2:41, 47	'Those who accepted his message were baptised, and about three thousand were added to their number that day.' 'And the Lord added to their number daily those who were being saved.' The Holy Spirit comes at Pentecost, enabling faithful witness.
4:4	'But many who heard the message believed, and the number of men grew to about five thousand.' As a result of their preaching, Peter and John are imprisoned, but many are converted.
6:7	'So the word of God spread. The number of disciples in Jerusalem increased rapidly, and a large number of priests became obedient to the faith.' The apostles give their attention to prayer and the ministry of the word. As a result, the word of God spreads.
9:31	'Then the church throughout Judea, Galilee and Samaria enjoyed a time of peace. It was strengthened; and encouraged by the Holy Spirit, it grew in numbers, living in the fear of the Lord.' This follows the conversion of Saul, who is to become the main instrument of Gentile mission outside of Judea and Samaria.
11:21	'The Lord's hand was with them, and a great number of people believed and turned to the Lord.' The beginning of witness in Antioch.
12:24	'But the word of God continued to increase and spread.' This statement follows Herod's persecution of the church (and his death!), ending the transitional period from Jerusalem to Antioch and ushering in the great age of mission.
13:43-44, 49	'When the congregation was dismissed, many of the Jews and devout converts to Judaism followed Paul and Barnabas, who talked with them and urged them to continue in the grace of God. On the next Sabbath almost the whole city gathered to hear the word of the Lord.' 'The word of the Lord spread through the whole region.' Paul and Barnabas in Pisidian Antioch.
14:21	'They preached the good news in that city and won a large number of disciples.' Paul and Barnabas in Derbe.
16:5	'So the churches were strengthened in the faith and grew daily in numbers.' This follows the Jerusalem Council's settlement of the issue of gospel purity, validating Gentile inclusion and the ongoing Gentile mission.
19:20	'In this way the word of the Lord spread widely and grew in power.' This signals the end of Paul's pioneer missionary activity. Ephesus was his last church plant; the word would continue to spread but no longer through Paul in this pioneering way.
28:23, 30	'They... came in even larger numbers to the place where [Paul] was staying... For two whole years Paul stayed there in his own rented house and welcomed all who came to see him.' This signals the end of the work recorded in Acts.

Narrative characteristics

The text of Acts embodies a number of narrative characteristics, which act as cues to the reader, revealing Luke's
purpose. These include the use of repetition, key words,
statistics and allocation of space. An overall focus of the
narrative can also be discerned. Some brief comments on
each.

(1) Repetition
Repetition is used to signal key events and identify major
turning points. Examples are:

(i) The coming of the Holy Spirit (chs. 2, 8, 10)
The coming of the Holy Spirit on the church to empower
its bold witness is so significant it is recorded three times.
In chapter 2 the Spirit comes on the Jewish church at
Pentecost. In chapter 8, through Peter and John, the Spirit
comes on the church in Samaria. In chapter 10, once again
through Peter, the Spirit comes on the Gentile, Cornelius,
and his family and close friends.

   Luke records the Spirit's coming three times to show that
the Samaritan and Gentile churches are in no way inferior
to the church in Jerusalem. It also shows that each church is
to boldly witness and that such bold witness has its source
in the baptism of the Spirit in the believer's life.

(ii) The conversion of Saul (chs. 9, 22, 26)
Saul's conversion and commissioning as the Apostle to
the Gentiles is recorded fully in chapter 9, repeated in its
entirety in chapter 22 to the crowd in Jerusalem, and then
again in chapter 26 to Festus and King Agrippa. Luke could
have referred the reader in chapters 22 and 26 to his earlier

account of Saul's conversion, but chooses not to. He repeats the full account in the narrative. The repetition emphasises the centrality of this event in the gospel's movement from Jerusalem to Rome.

(iii) The Gentile mission (ch. 10, 11, 15)

The gospel's reach to the Gentile world is recorded in God's dealing with Peter and Cornelius in chapter 10. This is then repeated to the Jerusalem apostles and brethren in chapter 11 and again referred to before the Jerusalem Council in chapter 15. Remember that before God's dealings with Peter in chapter 10, he and the other Jewish believers would have understood Luke 24:47 to read: '...and repentance and baptism of sins will be preached in his name to [*the Jews of*] all nations beginning at Jerusalem'. Luke shows that God's purpose is expansion 'to all nations' (Luke 24:47), i.e. 'to the ends of the earth (Acts 1:8).

(iv) The terms of Gentile inclusion in the church (ch. 15 [twice], 21)

The Jerusalem Council is such an important event in the narrative: here the church must decide whether Christianity is merely a new sect of Judaism or stands as a unique revelation. Does the gospel need to include circumcision, so that a Gentile must become a Jew first by circumcision before becoming a Christian? This is so vital that Luke records the letter of decision of the Council in Acts 15:19-21; again in Acts 15:23-29, and then records the Jerusalem leaders' reference to it in 21:25.

(v) 'The word of the Lord spread' (chs. 6, 12, 13, 19)

As discussed above, the phrase 'the word of the Lord spread', or similar, is used by Luke in Acts 6:7; 12:24, 13:49 and

19:20 to mark the key milestones in the spread of the gospel through Judea, Samaria, and into Gentile territory.

(2) *Key words*

Luke uses key words in his narrative to highlight where his emphasis lies. Examples are:

- the use of the *dei* ('it must happen') [this word is used over forty times in Luke/Acts (e.g. Luke 2:49; 4:43; 9:22; 17:25; 19:5; 21:9; 24:44; Acts 1:16; 3:21; 9:16; 17:3; 19:21; 23:11; 27:24)];
- the directional elements in chapter 1 (up, down, out);
- the direct words of God, the majority of which urge the church out to the next mission field (Acts 8:26; 9:6, 15; 10:19-20; 13:2; 16:9; 18:9-10; 20:22; 23:11; 27:24).

(3) *Statistics*

As indicated in Table 3 above, Luke uses statistics to emphasise the growth of the church.

(4) *Allocation of space*

Luke's allocation of space in his narrative reveals his relative interest. Two examples illustrate: the first, at the macro level, the second at the micro level.

Luke devotes one-third of his narrative (chapters 21-28) to Paul's torments and trials, indicating that, allied to the gospel's progress, is the inevitability of suffering and opposition. We read of the troubles Paul encountered in Jerusalem, in his trial before the Sanhedrin, before Felix and Festus, as well as his shipwreck and snakebite.

At the micro level, it is interesting to note the relative space devoted to the martyrdom of Stephen and James. Seventy-five verses are allocated to Stephen's martyrdom, with only one verse on James'. Why is this? Stephen's martyrdom was the catalyst for the gospel to spread out of Judea and led to the beginning of the Gentile mission; James' martyrdom had no discernable effect on the spread of the gospel.

(5) *Overall focus of the narrative*

Typical of Luke's Gospel account is that his interest is not primarily on the human characters involved. If Luke were the director of a television series you would sometimes want the camera to be elsewhere. For example, wouldn't you love to follow the demoniac from the region of the Gerasenes home to be reunited with his family (Luke 8:39), or to have been at home with the family of the little girl raised from the dead as they sat for their first family meal following her death and resurrection (Luke 8:53-55)? But Luke's focus is relentlessly on Jesus. Different characters cross his path, are changed profoundly, and move on, but the camera remains on Jesus!

The same is true of Acts. We would love to go home with the Ethiopian treasurer, to see how differently he now administers the treasury. We want to see how the families of Cornelius, or the Philippian jailer, develop after their conversions. We are intrigued as to how Sergius Paulus will operate as a Christian proconsul. But again, Luke is relentlessly focused on the gospel. It comes via the human messenger, touches people profoundly and then moves on to its next encounter.

Luke's purpose is to show the gospel reaching out, carried by Spirit-empowered messengers, under God's superintendence, to Jew, Samaritan and Gentile. This is the melody of Acts: the fulfilment of God's plan to gather in his people from the far reaches of the earth. Christ is ascended, but he continues to direct his church and empower it through his Spirit. This is why the book of Acts has been a great encouragement to gospel-bearers through the centuries.

Purpose of Acts

For good reason the book of Acts has been called a fertile seedbed of schism. Much dissension arises from differences in opinion over Luke's purpose in writing Acts. Did Luke write in order to justify some experience of the Holy Spirit in salvation? Did he write to provide a model of church government through the ages? Or was it to provide a Biblical foundation for some views of water baptism? In other words, does Luke write to provide us with a church manual?

Luke was an historian. In Luke 1:1-4 he makes it clear that his purpose is to provide an orderly account, based on careful investigation. He records facts like the birth, life, death, resurrection and ascension of Jesus. But this is no dry history! He engages our emotions. There is humour in the angelic kick to the body of the snoozing Peter (12:7) and in Rhoda's excited neglect of Peter's knocking at the door of Mary's house (12:14). We are moved by the tears of the Ephesian elders as they bid farewell to Paul for the last time (20:36-38). We are angered by the underhand ways of the envious opponents, the Jews, who would rather leave pagans in paganism than see them come to Christ (14:19). We are appalled at the miserable Felix waiting for his bribe, leaving Paul to suffer in prison (24:26). And our hearts are warmed at every mention of the encourager, Barnabas (4:36; 9:27; 11:25; 15:36-39). But while Luke involves his readers emotionally, his key interest is in showing us why things happened the way they did.

(1) Fulfilment of God's plans

God is the sovereign Lord of history. He is the faithful God. Things happen in fulfilment of God's plan. Central here is Luke 24:46-47 and Acts 1:8. These are the bridging verses connecting volumes 1 and 2.

Verse 46 is a good summary of Luke's Gospel, while verse 47 is a good summary of Acts. It is helpful to quote the verses in full here, since this is such an important point:

> LUKE: 'He told them, "This is what is written: The Christ will suffer and rise   from the dead on the third day…"' (Luke 24:46)

> ACTS: "…and repentance and forgiveness of sins will be preached in his name to all nations, beginning at Jerusalem" (Luke 24:47).

Verse 47 is as much the purpose of God as verse 46. To take one without the other makes no sense. The plan of God is the salvation of the nations. Jesus is the one to carry out this plan through his birth, death and resurrection, and then by his Holy Spirit empowering the church to reach the nations from Jerusalem to the ends of the earth. Acts 1:7-8: 'He said to them, "It is not for you to know the times or dates the Father has set by his own authority. But you will receive power when the Holy Spirit comes on you; and you will be my witnesses in Jerusalem, and in all Judea and Samaria and to the ends of the earth."'

(2) God at work

God is clearly at work right from the outset in Acts. He accredited Jesus (2:22-23). He made this Jesus both Lord and Christ (2:36). He calls his people to salvation (2:39). Jesus is active, speaking to Paul on the Damascus Road (9:4-5), disallowing Paul from entering Bithynia (16:7) and encouraging Paul in Corinth (18:9-10). The Holy Spirit is active, baptizing the believers in chapter 2, filling them again in 4:31, coming on the Gentiles in 10:44-45 and setting apart the missionaries in 13:2.

God is actively bringing about the fulfilment of his plan. And because it is God's plan, it will be fulfilled! It is an unstoppable gospel, despite:

+ external religious opposition (4:1ff; 5:17ff; 6:8ff);
+ economic opposition (16:16ff; 19:23ff);
+ internal hypocrisy (5:1ff);
+ church friction (6:1-7; 15:36-41);
+ persecution (5:17ff; 8:1ff; 12:1ff; 13:49-52; 14:19-20; 17:1ff; 21:27ff);
+ martyrdom (7:54-8:4; 12:1-4);
+ storms and shipwrecks (27:13ff);
+ courts (4:5ff; 18:12-17; 24:1ff; 25:1ff);
+ imprisonment (12:5ff; 16:16ff);
+ orthodox religious tradition (15:1ff).

God will see his plan through! Christ will bring his people to salvation! Repentance and forgiveness of sins will be preached in his name to all nations! The gospel will reach the ends of the earth! It is written!

(3) Focus on Jesus

The gospel is all about the Lord Jesus Christ (Acts 1:1; 2:36, 38; 4:8-12; 5:42; 8:12, 35; 10:36; 11:20-21; 13:38-39; 15:11; 16:31; 18:5, 28; 19:4; 20:24; 24:24; 28:31).

Luke also makes it clear what it's not about:

+ It's not about Judaism (15:10).
+ It's not about spiritism (16:18).

+ It's not about politics (17:7).
+ It's not about philosophy (17:18).

It is the broadcast of this gospel about Jesus Christ which God uses to bring about the fulfilment of his purpose. And therefore, the focus of preaching in Acts is Jesus:

+ At Pentecost Peter preaches about Jesus (2:14-39).
+ At the healing of the lame man, Peter preaches about Jesus (3:6).
+ To the God-fearing, Peter preaches Jesus (10:34-48).
+ To conservative Jews, the apostles preach Jesus (14:3).
+ To sophisticated Greeks, Paul preaches Jesus (17:31).
+ To disciples of John the Baptist, Paul preaches Jesus (19:4).
+ Jesus is preached as the Christ (2:31, 36, 38; 3:6, 18, 20; 4:10; 5:42; 8:5; 9:22; 10:36; 16:18; 17:3; 18:5, 28; 26:23; 28:31), son of David (2:25-36; 4:25-26; 13:33-34), Son of Man (7:56), Lord (1:6; 2:21, 36; 7:59-60; 9:5; 10:36), author of life (3:15), leader and Saviour (5:31; 13:23), prophet like Moses (3:22; 7:37), holy and righteous one (2:27; 3:14; 7:52; 22:14).

(4) Jesus and his Church

Luke is also concerned to show the continuity between Jesus in Luke and his church in Acts. For example, there are clear parallels between the prophetic voices of Simeon and Anna at the time of Jesus' birth (Luke 2:25-38) and Peter's reference to the prophetic fulfilment of Joel (Acts 2:17-21) at the birth of the church. The flow of the gospel in Luke is Christ towards Jerusalem. In Acts, it is from Jerusalem out to the world. Each volume begins with a similar introduction to Theophilus, a period of waiting and prayer (1:1-14; cf. Luke 1:1-56) and then the coming of the Spirit (on Jesus at his baptism, and upon his church at Pentecost).

(5) Jesus and Paul

There are also clear parallels between the Lord Jesus and Paul:

+ Both come to Jerusalem and after a good initial reception are rejected by the people (Luke 19:37-40; Acts 21:17-20).
+ Both visit the temple (Luke 19:45-47; Acts 21:26).
+ Both are opposed by the Sadducees (Luke 20:27ff; Acts 23:6-8).
+ Both are seized by the mob (Luke 22:47-54; Acts 21:30-36).
+ Both are struck by the High Priest's officials (John 18:22; Acts 23:2).
+ Both experience four trials (Luke 22:66; 23:1, 7, 13; Acts 22:30; 24:1; 25:1ff, 23).

Applying Acts today

We must apply Acts in a way that is consistent with Luke's purpose. Our task is to focus on what is important to him.

(1) God's mission heart

The character of God will be central, and in particular, his heart for the lost. Moreover, God is instrumental in directing his people in mission. For example, he deals with Peter's reluctance to go to Cornelius' house. He oversees the sensitive appointment of Barnabas to Antioch. He guides James at the Jerusalem Council. He superintends the scattering of believers to Samaria following Stephen's death. He urges the setting apart of Barnabas and Saul for missionary work. He sends the vision of the man of Macedonia to Paul, and thus brings the gospel to Europe.

(2) *Gospel progress*

The progress of the gospel is inevitable, despite many obstacles. The gospel messenger is not promised an easy road. Jesus' messiahship involved him taking up a cross. And the pattern for the disciple, whether the apostle Paul, or you and me, is cross-bearing. For every Christian, the life of discipleship is cross-shaped.

(3) *The empowering Spirit*

The presence of the empowering Holy Spirit in the life of the church is emphasised. All that is accomplished is due to his direct involvement in transforming those who were once self-centred and insecure into outgoing, courageous and sacrificial servants of the gospel. All forms of ministry are affirmed: the preacher, the one-to-one evangelist, the ministry of table service, the discipler of new believers leading them to a better grasp of the truth, and those who make clothes for the poor. Moreover, both men and women are affirmed in their gospel ministry.

All these issues, close to Luke's heart, are fertile grounds for application to the church of the twenty-first century, as it battles to maintain its integrity in a secular, Godless world.

(4) *God's sovereignty in a hostile world*

The proclamation of the gospel in a society which enshrines tolerance above all else, makes persecution inevitable. Despite the persecution, however, God is sovereign, directing the progress of the gospel and protecting his people. God will *inevitably* bring his purposes to fulfilment. Consider these verses:

+ 'So then, God has granted even the Gentiles repentance unto life' (11:18).
+ '... and all who were appointed for eternal life believed' (13:48).
+ 'The Lord opened her heart to respond to Paul's message' (16:14).
+ 'For I am with you, and no one is going to attack and harm you, because I have many people in this city' (18:10).

The obvious hope for society, then as now, is that the Word of the gospel is preached. Luke shows how this gospel transforms lives from Jerusalem to Rome. God constantly exhorts the church in this vital task of proclamation. Of the twenty-two direct words of divine speech in Acts (i.e. where Jesus, the Lord, the Holy Spirit, a voice, or an angel speak) sixteen are reminders to the church of the need to keep reaching out to the ends of the earth. Reflecting on this in his commentary, Blaiklock comments: '...to press outward from the fringe is always sound policy, provided it is done with vigour and devotion' (*Tyndale Commentary*, E.M. Blaiklock, 1967, p. 50).

Pastoral impact

Luke's pastoral interest is seen in his concern that Theophilus and others should have 'certainty' of what they have been taught (Luke 1:4). Doubt paralyses and Acts is an antidote to doubt. Invariably, doubt springs from unrealistic expectations, and so the book of Acts delivers a healthy dose of reality to believers. This is why Dr Lloyd-Jones said:

'Live in that book, I exhort you; it is a tonic, the greatest tonic I know of in the realm of the Spirit' (Lloyd-Jones, *The Christian Warfare* (Banner of Truth, 1976), p. 274).

My daughter and son-in-law are missionaries in Mongolia. In 1992, Mongolia became independent of the Soviet Union, and with religious freedom, the church has flourished. Mongolians don't give their trust easily. For over seventy years as part of the USSR no one knew who could be trusted. The big issue for the believer in Mongolia is whether or not God can be trusted to deliver on his promises. One of the threats to the young Mongolian church is prosperity preachers from the West who tell converts they can expect health and wealth from God. While God can be trusted absolutely, he cannot be trusted to deliver on a promise he has never made.

Luke, therefore, is careful to deliver his readers from the anxiety that arises from false pessimism as well as the unreal excitement that arises from false optimism. There is no false triumphalism here. Gospel workers can expect a difficult time. As already noted, one-third of Acts (chs. 21-28) covers Paul's troubles. In fact, whatever speech or event, the inevitable pattern in Acts is a divided response. 'The people of the city were divided; some sided with the Jews, others with the apostles' (14:4). 'When they heard about the resurrection from the dead, some of them sneered, but others said, "We want to hear you again on this subject." ... A few men became followers of Paul and believed ...' (17:32-34).

Acts has sobering words for advocates of a prosperity gospel. 'I will show him how much he must suffer for my name' (9:16). '"We must go through many hardships to enter the kingdom of God"' (14:22). 'I only know that in every city the Holy Spirit warns me that prison and hardships are facing me' (20:23).

Remember the words of the Lord Jesus in John 16:33, 'In this world you will have trouble. But take heart! I have overcome the world'. His guarantee is that we can expect trouble in this world, but also peace in the midst of it. This is the experience of those who rest in Christ. Acts, therefore, is a great encouragement to keep going, as we seek to communicate the gospel faithfully in a hostile world. The gospel is the world's only hope, and we must not be silenced. No matter how tough things are, the gospel will not be overcome. 'God buries his workmen, but carries on his work' (John Wesley).

Luke chooses his last words well! In Luke 1:4 (the end of the introduction to Luke-Acts) the last word in the Greek text is 'certainty'. In Acts 28:31 the last word is (literally) 'unhinderedly', a dynamic adverb modifying the participles 'preaching' and 'teaching'. In other words, Acts is the end of the beginning. The God of mission lives. He empowers his people now as then. The unconverted are converted through the preaching of the gospel. *Dei* – 'It must happen!' Acts shows us the triumph of God's purpose.

To be apostolic today is to see the world and to respond to it as the apostles did. It is to imitate the apostolic character, to preach the apostolic gospel and to follow Jesus as part of God's plan and kingdom. To be committed to that plan and its fulfilment is always the mandate of the apostolic church. The extent to which a church commits itself to this missionary task is the extent to which it could be said to be Christian. Jerusalem, to Samaria, to the ends of the earth remains our mandate!

2

PLANNING A SERIES ON ACTS

A suggested series

Acts could be divided into three major series of sermons around these three main movements:

+ Chapters 1-7, The gospel at work in Jerusalem and Judea.
+ Chapters 8-12, The gospel at work in Samaria.
+ Chapters 13-28, The gospel at work in Gentile territory.

Series 1. A Great Tonic! (Acts 1:1-6:7)

Week 1	Introductory Sermon: 'Tonic For Your Soul: Why This Will Be Good For You'	Luke 1:1-4; Acts 1:1-2; Luke 24:46-49; Acts 1:3-8
Week 2	'Will Things Be Different? Yes And No!'	Acts 1:1-26
Week 3	'How To Be Fully And Forever Equipped'	Acts 2:1-13; 8:14-17
Week 4	'It's All About Jesus'	Acts 2:14-47
Week 5	'The Triumphant Indicative'	Acts 3
Week 6	'Handling Hostility' 'Who Pulls The Strings And Who Speaks The Truth'	Acts 4:1-31; 5:17-42
Week 7	'Telling Lies To God'	Acts 4:32-5:11
Week 8	'So The Word Of God Spread'	Acts 6:1-7

Series 2. The Word Spreads! (Acts 6:8-13:3)

Week 1	'The Church's First Martyr'	Acts 6:8-8:1
Week 2	'The Story Of One: Expansion To Samaria'	Acts 8:26-40
Week 3	'A Surprising Conversion'	Acts 9:1-20; 22:1-22; 26:1-32
Week 4	'God's Expansive Purposes'	Acts 10:1-11:18
Week 5	'The Hidden Hand At Work'	Acts 12:1-25
Week 6	'Our Mother Church'	Acts 11:19-30; 13:1-3

Series 3. The Unstoppable Gospel! (Acts 13:4-28:31)

Week 1	'What's In A Name?'	Acts 13:4-14:28
Week 2	'Things Which Go Without Saying'	Acts 15:1-16:5
Week 3	'The Five City Tour'	Acts 16:6-18:22
Week 4	'A Model Ministry'	Acts 18:23-20:38
Week 5	'O Jerusalem, Jerusalem'	Acts 21:1-23:24
Week 6	'Trial Upon Trial'	Acts 23:25-26:32
Week 7	'Through Many Dangers, Toils And Snares'	Acts 27:1-28:10
Week 8	'Unhinderedly'	Acts 28:11-31

These series might be preached consecutively, or as separate series with a break in between. If they are tackled separately, it would be useful to recap on the material in the introductory sermon (Series 1) at the start of Series 2 and 3.

Structure of the chapters which follow

This suggested structure forms the basis of the chapters which follow. A separate chapter is devoted to each sermon/ Bible study.

Individual chapters follow a consistent structure or methodology, specifically geared to help you get to grips with the text, in order to teach it: 'listening to the text', 'from text to teaching' and 'proclaiming the message'. Some brief comments on this methodology will be helpful by way of navigation.

(1) *Listening to the text*

Listening to the text is the right kind of engagement with biblical text. It is a careful and methodical activity, but never a forensic exercise! In his book, *Working the Angles*, Eugene Peterson reminds us that we approach the inspired Word of God, not as cool analysts, but as passionate hearers! The former approach will have us taking a tool kit to the text; the latter (and right approach) will first find us prayerfully meditating on the text (Ps. 1) and then, appropriately and sensitively, picking up our analytical tools. In human interaction, we learn most by asking the right questions and listening patiently to the answers. The careful reader of Scripture will ask questions like:

+ What is the author saying?
+ Why does he say it like this?
+ Why does he say it like this in this context?
+ What did it mean to the first readers?
+ What does it mean now?
+ What should I do about it?
+ What pictures is he using?

All these are useful questions to guide reflection. Your own personal discoveries will lead to a more passionate presentation and a renewed freshness in your preaching. The saying is true:

+ A truth taught is interesting.
+ A truth caught is exciting and challenging.
+ A truth discovered is life-changing.

In the chapters that follow, the content of the section 'listening to the text', will vary according to the nature and dynamics of the particular passage being studied.

Having engaged with the text in this way, it would then be appropriate to consult the commentaries.

(2) From text to teaching

By the end of step (1) we should have got to grips with the essentials of the passage. As we sit at our desk, we have a 'text to explain'. If that is the end point, however, our preaching will sound like a lecture or commentary. To preach or teach a passage we must move beyond a 'text to explain' to having a 'message to proclaim'. It's good to keep the logic of this discipline clear in our working week. By Thursday we should have a 'text to explain', but by Sunday we must have a 'message to proclaim'. This is a simplistic illustration, I know, but it makes an important point!

A number of steps can be identified in this movement from text to teaching. Again, these are not prescriptive, but simply a template or guide to the kind of process we should be working through.

(i) Get the message clear

Our concern here is to nail down the essential message of the text. If you like, it is to separate the boulder from the rocks and pebbles in a passage. A helpful way to get the message clear is to identify the big idea and then conceptualize that idea as a question or questions. The terms 'theme' (theme sentence) and 'aim' (aim sentence) are often used, but personally I find 'idea' and 'question' easier to work with. If our preaching is to be engaging then all our sermons must answer a question and it must be the question answered by the passage. I try to state the big idea of the passage in one succinct sentence. The big question takes the statement of the big idea and turns it into a question. The preacher will then spend the early part of the sermon showing why the big question is important and relevant for his listeners.

For example, if I were preaching on Matthew 6:24, the big idea would be: 'The citizen of the Kingdom must follow God not wealth, not God and wealth.' Appropriate questions would be:

+ Why not worship wealth?
+ Who is truly God?
+ Why follow God?
+ How do we avoid divided allegiance?

In determining the big question or questions, each one should be tested against the passage in order to determine whether it is being answered by the passage. If I set a big question which is not obviously answered by the passage, then it will lead to confusion!

(ii) Engage the hearer

Two issues are of central relevance here: what I call 'point of contact' and 'dominant picture(s) / illustration(s).

By point of contact (sometimes called 'hook'), my intention is to immediately connect the passage into the lives of the listeners. I think of my sermon as a 747 jumbo jet! It requires maximum thrust to get it off the ground and maximum thrust to land. I give a lot of attention to both the introduction and conclusion of the sermon. I always begin with life, never the Bible, and then bring the life situation to the Bible. To repeat what others have said: to get to first century Palestine, I start my listeners at Sydney airport and get them back (always a return ticket, never one-way!). In terms of an appropriate point of contact, a helpful gauge is to think whether it connects with the big question.

It is always helpful to use illustrations in sermons or Bible studies, but only if they are good illustrations! Too often, the connection with the point being illustrated is tenuous. Illustrations must never be used for their own sake, but only if they clarify the point. A good way to work on illustration is first to determine the dominant picture(s) in a passage and then work on illustration by filling out that picture.

(iii) Work on application

As I noted in the Preface, issues of application are always difficult! Application, however, is vitally important. Fundamentally, our confidence is in the living inspired Word. Scripture necessarily implicates the passage in the life of the hearer and implicates the life of the hearer in the passage. It's not our job to make the passage applied, but to apply the passage!

I work on application at three levels. The first is the **necessary application** - how the passage must apply to all hearers at all times. This is the authoritative application, calling on people to repent of some specific attitude or action and to trust in Christ in a specific way.

The opposite of the necessary is the **impossible application** (the second level of application) i.e. how the passage cannot possibly apply. I assume that over half of my listeners are living consistently with the impossible application of the passage! Therefore I try to confront the impossible application directly and refute it. For example, in Matthew 6:24 Jesus begins: 'No one can' and concludes 'You can not' serve both God and wealth. Twice in the one verse he stresses that we cannot serve two masters, God and wealth. The necessary application is to recognise that God is God, repent of our service of wealth and follow him. We must not substitute wealth for God. The impossible application of that verse is to think that we are the exception, and that we *can* serve two masters. In my experience, it is always good for the preacher to point out how the passage cannot be understood. It's a great way of exposing what people are really thinking!

The third level is the **possible application**. How might the teaching of this passage work out personally? How might the passage apply, at some time and in some circumstances, to some people? By showing how the passage applies for himself or others, the preacher is suggesting ways of practical application. For example, financial generosity is one way of showing God's Lordship over wealth. Some people look on a tithe (ten percent of income) as a good guide to giving. Some look on a tithe as the equivalent of paying taxes, and giving starts after the 10 percent. The preacher must be careful not to push the possible application up to the level of the necessary application and therefore make his insights (rather than the truths explicitly taught in the text) the basis of a call for repentance. The tithe must not become the necessary application of this passage.

(3) *Proclaiming the message*

The third section in each chapter is 'proclaiming the message'. I have included a suggested preaching outline and format for leading a Bible study. These, of course, are simply my suggestions - make use of them as you think best. The Bible study works through four logical steps, which I have found helpful as a general format.

+ Step 1: Introduce the issues
+ Step 2: Study the passage
+ Step 3: Think it through
+ Step 4: Live it out

SERIES ONE:

A Great Tonic!

Acts 1:1-6:7

3

INTRODUCTORY SERMON

'Tonic For Your Soul: Why This Will Be Good For You'
(LUKE 1:1-4; ACTS 1:1-2; LUKE 24:46-49; ACTS 1:3-8)

Rather than begin the series by diving straight into Acts 1 as the first sermon or Bible study, there will be value in taking time to prepare your hearers for the series. As a general point, it is always good to remind folk of the value of a systematic expository approach to a book of the Bible. And for this particular series, it is important to establish Luke's purpose in providing the historical account which is Acts. An introductory study will help people put the book in its historical context as well as whetting their appetite for what follows.

Listening to the text
(1) Why did Luke write (Luke 1:1-4; Acts 1:1-2)?
A preaching series on Acts must begin with Luke's Gospel. Luke introduces his Gospel in Luke 1:1-4 and then provides a similar, if briefer, introduction in Acts 1:1-2. The introduction to Acts shows that Luke's purpose is to provide a follow-on account from his Gospel of what Jesus *continued* to do and teach from His ascension onwards.

From Luke 1:1-4 the following points need to be made:

- Luke records the outworking of God's plan; 'things that have been fulfilled' (v. 1).
- His reliable sources are eyewitnesses and servants of the Word (v. 2).
- He has 'carefully investigated everything' (v. 3).
- He provides a well-ordered chronological account (v. 3).
- He wants to assure Theophilus of the reliability of these things and so to have certainty (v. 4).

(2) The bridge between Luke and Acts (Luke 24:46-49; Acts 1:3-8)

Luke wanted Theophilus to be clear about the certain fulfilment of God's purposes (Luke 24:46-49). Specifically, he has three points of fulfilment in mind. First, that Christ suffered, died and rose from the dead (v. 46); second, that repentance and forgiveness of sins will be preached to all nations (v. 47); and third, that power for witness will come through the Holy Spirit (vv. 48-49). These same three points are made in Acts 1:3-8, but in the order 1, 3, 2 (i.e. 'Christ suffered, died and rose', 'power for witness through the Spirit', 'the gospel to all nations'). The link between the end of Luke and the beginning of Acts is indisputable.

(i) Christ suffered, died and rose from the dead (Luke 24:46; Acts 1:3)

'The Christ will suffer and rise from the dead on the third day'. Luke 24:46 reminds us that 'this is what is written', that the suffering, death and resurrection of Jesus are the things to be fulfilled. Luke underlines this in Acts 1:3, reminding

Theophilus that Christ 'presented himself alive after his suffering by many proofs'.

In Luke 24:47 Christ makes it clear to the disciples that an imperative flows from these things, namely that 'repentance and forgiveness of sins should be proclaimed in his name.' The question is: to whom should this message be proclaimed?

(ii) The gospel to all nations (Luke 24:47; Acts 1:6-8)

Jesus continues: 'to all nations, beginning at Jerusalem' (Luke 24:47). Luke reminds us that God expects and oversees the preaching to all nations of repentance and forgiveness of sins in Christ's name. These, too, are the things to be fulfilled, and presumably featured in the teaching Jesus gave his disciples in the forty days between his resurrection and ascension (Acts 1:3). Yet it would appear that even after this period of privileged teaching from the resurrected Lord, the apostles still do not understand that his kingdom will embrace all nations. They ask: 'Lord, will you at this time restore the kingdom to Israel?' (Acts 1:6). Jesus' reply challenges their parochialism. He lifts their sights from their own backyard to the farthest reaches of the earth by telling them '...you will be my witnesses in Jerusalem and in all Judea and Samaria, and to the end of the earth' (Acts 1:8b).

This needs to be emphasised in our day. It is as much the purpose of God that Luke 24:47 be fulfilled as it was his purpose that verse 46 be fulfilled. It is vitally important that we commit ourselves to preaching the gospel, to broadcasting it as widely as possible, because God has declared this to be his purpose. As Wesley said: 'Parochialism is always the enemy of the gospel, and unchecked we will naturally be parochial.' Luke 24:47 is designed to upset our limited evangelistic interests. And lest we think that verse 47 is a one-off, we should note that substantial sections of the first and last books of the Bible stress God's love for the nations. Recent surveys have shown that most people having tea or coffee after church on Sunday morning commonly remember the first thing the preacher said, the last thing, and any big mistakes made in between! Maybe God's perfect knowledge of our human nature accounts for Scripture being bookended with statements of his intention to be made known among the nations. Consider these two passages.

Genesis 12:2-3: 'I will make you into a great nation and I will bless you … and all peoples on earth will be blessed through you.' Whenever Paul was speaking to Jews and God-fearers (e.g. in synagogues in Pisidian Antioch, Acts 13:26) he alludes to the availability of the message of salvation through Abraham's descendents.

Revelation 5:9-10: 'You are worthy to take the scroll and to open its seals, because you were slain, and with your blood you purchased men for God from every tribe and language and people and nation. You have made them to be a kingdom and priests to serve our God, and they will reign on the earth.'

Clearly, mission is at the heart of God's purpose, because its fruit brings honour to his Son. And his Son must be honoured. The kingdom of this earth is to be the kingdom of the Son. It is this truth – that Christ should receive the honour due to his Name from all the nations – that is the highest motivation for evangelism. It will come about through the preaching of the gospel by his appointed witnesses. His proclamation must continue until he returns as glorified King. It must continue despite the certainty of suffering for those who proclaim the gospel.

(iii) The Apostles and the Spirit (Luke 24:48-49; Acts 1:4-5)
Luke 24:48-49 makes it clear that the apostles are the witnesses to this gospel and that God will clothe them for the task 'with power from on high' so that they can carry out the task of proclaiming it. In Acts 1:4-5 Luke reminds his readers that the apostles' baptism by the Spirit will fulfil the promise made about Christ by John the Baptist in Luke 3:16. When they receive the Holy Spirit it will clearly be the outworking of God's plan.

Jesus continues to instruct the apostles in Acts 1:6-7, showing them that their primary concern is not to be the restoration of Israel but the reception of the Holy Spirit. Acts 1:8 is the climax - the Holy Spirit will empower the apostles. His power is purposeful - it is the power for witness. Such witness will take the apostles further and further out - to Jerusalem, to the furthest corners of Judea, into Samaria and then beyond.

(3) God's plan worked out - two examples
The apostles never lost this sense of being commissioned by God to proclaim the gospel as his Spirit-empowered witnesses - see Acts 5:29, 32; 10:42. Their Lord's last command to them was their first concern. Let's look at two examples.

(i) The Spirit-empowered boldness of Peter and John
First, Acts 4:13ff. The Sanhedrin, which had persecuted the Lord Jesus, calls Peter and John to explain the healing of the beggar in chapter 3. Here is the cowering Peter of

the Gospels now 'on the front foot', declaring that Jesus is responsible for the healing (v. 10), that he is the rejected capstone (v. 11) and that salvation is not to be found through the law, but in him. Even the Sanhedrin note their courage and insight (v. 13), recognising that it is due to Peter's and John's association with Jesus. Spurgeon has said: '…the best life of Christ is his living biography, written out in the words and actions of his people' (*Morning and Evening*, Feb 11, AM).

Luke makes the point clear: 'Peter, filled with the Holy Spirit, said to them…"there is no other name under heaven given to men by which we must be saved"' (vv. 8, 12). Peter is as he is because the Spirit of God is empowering him to declare Christ as Lord and Saviour.

(ii) The Spirit-empowered boldness of Stephen

The second example of this kind of God-empowered boldness is Stephen (Acts 6). Stephen is described as a man 'full of faith and the Holy Spirit' (v. 5), 'full of God's grace and power' (v. 8). He is elected to a position requiring fullness 'of the Spirit and wisdom' (v. 3). Jesus has promised the disciples the help of the Holy Spirit when they are brought before the authorities (Luke 12:11-12). We see a fulfilment of that promise here as the Spirit empowers Stephen for clear and bold proclamation. Though seemingly the one on trial, Stephen declares that it is the Sanhedrin, as the representatives of Israel, who are on trial before God himself! This is a powerful reminder that unenlightened intellect is never a match for Spirit-empowered testimony.

Rather than removing Stephen from the danger that such an audacious charge puts him in, the Spirit gives Stephen the courage to remain faithful to Christ even to death. His Christ-likeness is most obvious when he prays as Jesus did at His crucifixion, except that Stephen addresses Jesus, rather than the Father, as God: 'Lord Jesus, receive my spirit' (v. 59 – cf. Luke 23:46). Here we see another role the Spirit plays in the lives of his witnesses – to give them perseverance through suffering while they faithfully testify to the gospel.

From text to teaching
(1) Get the message clear
Big idea (theme)
It is God's purpose that his gospel be preached to the ends of the earth by Holy Spirit empowered preachers.

Big question(s) (aim)
Preaching or teaching on this passage should answer the following questions:

+ What is God's purpose?
+ Why has God given his Holy Spirit?
+ What's on God's mind?
+ What is it that is closest to God's heart?

(2) Engage the hearer
Point of contact
What effect do tonics have on you? Illustrate by referring to some tonic or other, citing the health benefits on the label. This is an appropriate point of contact for showing why Acts is God's spiritual tonic. Remember Dr Lloyd-Jones' quote: 'Live in that book, I exhort you; it is a tonic, the greatest tonic I know of in the realm of the Spirit.' (Lloyd-Jones, *The Christian Warfare* [Banner of Truth, 1976], p. 274).

Dominant picture(s)

'This is what is written' – the finger of God has inscribed words that will never depreciate, erode or be changed. Aboriginal rock art, ancient manuscripts, museum artefacts stored in soft light and touched only by gloved hands, modern writing in 'permanent' ink, graffiti, even words recorded on digital media – all will fade or become corrupted. But God's Word and God's purposes stand forever. They never fade! His words have been, are being, and will be fulfilled.

(3) Work on application

Necessary application(s)

God has promised that salvation would be proclaimed 'to the ends of the earth' (Isaiah 49:6). Jesus confirms this promise in his last words to the disciples (Acts 1:8), and this purpose becomes their first concern. God empowers his first century witnesses by the Holy Spirit to be faithful and bold preachers of the gospel, so that by the end of Acts, the gospel is being proclaimed in Rome, the heart of Gentile territory. So Acts is written to give us certainty that God's plans are always fulfilled. Do we have confidence in this? Will that confidence lead us and our church to be vitally involved in God's continuing missionary endeavour?

Luke 24:46-49 and Acts 1:1-8 build trust in God, erode self-confidence and widen our vision. It was said of Wesley: 'the world was his parish'. The world is God's parish and it is to be ours as well. These words should revitalise our memories. They should help us to remember the things that are important – things we all too easily forget. Denominational boundaries, ethnic boundaries, social, economic, language, geographical, political boundaries are all immaterial because the world is God's interest and so should be ours. His concerns are to be our concerns. Drink this down – it is tonic for our souls! It is good for us. If the world is God's concern, if it is the anguish of his heart, if it is his parish, then it should be ours as well.

Refute impossible application(s)

The impossible application for the individual Christian or Christian fellowship is that they are excused from participating in God's mission. The progress of the gospel does not stop with us! A church that claims to be Christian yet has no concern to get the gospel beyond its doors is not a Christian church.

Possible application(s)

God will use my testimony in all its frailty to glorify himself by bringing people to trust in his Son. I am not to trust in the gift of the gab, but in God, the great evangelist, to do his work through me. Physical fitness is a matter of building muscles and losing fat. Spiritual fitness builds my trust in God to do His work and weakens my trust in my own sufficiency. Acts helps us to see that self-sufficiency is insufficiency.

Do I show enough confidence in the Holy Spirit to step out and witness? When I speak, I find that people are more ready to hear than I have been to speak. The Bible draws a connection between what is on the heart, and what is expressed by the tongue. What we believe in our hearts will find its way to the tongue (Luke 6:45; Rom. 10:9). I must not be silent; a consistent life is vital but it is not enough; I must speak.

Proclaiming the message
A preaching outline

Title: 'Tonic For Your Soul: Why This Will Be Good For You'

Texts: Luke 1:1-4; Acts 1:1-2; Luke 24:46-49; Acts 1:3-8

(1) **Why Luke wrote (Luke 1:1-4; Acts 1:1-2)**

Luke 1:1-4

Acts 1:1-2

(2) **The bridge between Luke and Acts (Luke 24:46-49; Acts 1:3-8)**

- Christ suffered, died and rose from the dead (Luke 24:46)
- The gospel to all nations (Luke 24:47)
- The Holy Spirit - power for witness (Luke 24:48-49)
- Christ suffered, died and rose from the dead (Acts 1:3)
- The Holy Spirit – power for witness (Acts 1:4-5)
- The gospel to all nations (Acts 1:6-8)

(3) **God's plan worked out – two examples**

Example 1: The Spirit-empowered boldness of Peter and John (Acts 4:13ff)

Example 2: The Spirit-empowered boldness of Stephen (Acts 6:10ff)

(4) **Tonic for your soul**

- Acts will strengthen your trust
- Acts will weaken your pride
- Acts will widen your vision
- Acts will revitalise your memory

Leading a Bible study

Title: 'Tonic For Your Soul: Why This Will Be Good
For You'

Texts: Luke 1:1-4; Acts 1:1-2; Luke 24:46-49; Acts 1:3-8

(1) Introduce the issues

John Wesley said: 'Parochialism is always the enemy of the
gospel.' Discuss what he meant and investigate how parochialism might be evident today.

(2) Study the passages

Luke 1:1-4; Acts 1:1-3

i)   Why do you think it is significant that Luke writes
     about things being fulfilled (Luke 1:1)?

ii) What has Luke provided for Theophilus so that he
     might have certainty (Luke 1:2-4; Acts 1:3)?

iii) How does Luke consider the book of Acts to be related
     to his Gospel (Acts 1:1)?

Luke 24:46-49

iv) What is the significance of Jesus' use of the introduction,
     'This is what is written…' (v. 46)? (see also Luke 4:4;
     4:8; 4:10; 19:46; 21:22; 22:37).

v)   According to these verses, what must happen in order
     for the purposes of God to be fulfilled?

Acts 1:4-8

vi) What does Jesus promise to his disciples?

vii) What is the Holy Spirit's power intended to do for the
     disciples?

viii) What do you notice about Jerusalem, Judea, Samaria
      and the ends of the earth as a geographical pattern?

ix)   How do Luke 24:46-47 and Acts 1:8 provide a bridge
      from Luke's first volume, his Gospel, to Acts, his
      second volume?

(3) Think it through

i)   In his commentary on Acts, Blaiklock comments: 'To
      press outward from the fringe is always sound policy,
      provided it is done with vigour and devotion.' Discuss
      this as a response to Acts 1:8.

ii)   Parochialism is confinement. How does this statement
      by Blaiklock and the verses we have looked at in this
      study confront parochialism?

(4) Live it out

i)   What are the implications of studying these passages,
      both for us as individuals, and corporately as a church?

ii)   How can we encourage each other to press outward
      from the fringe with the gospel?

iii) How will this affect our giving, our praying and how
      we live our lives?

iv)   As a church, how do we identify the fringe and press
      beyond it with vigour and devotion?

v)   Where is our fringe now?

4

'WILL THINGS BE DIFFERENT? YES AND NO!'

(ACTS 1:1-26)

Listening to the text
(1) Context and structure

Before his ascension, Jesus gave convincing proofs that he was alive. Eating and drinking together was one aspect that seemed to have stood out for Peter. Luke 24:42-43: 'They gave him a piece of broiled fish, and he took it and ate it in their presence'. And here in Acts 1:4, Luke again records the apostles sharing in table fellowship with the risen Lord. In this graphic way Jesus is showing the disciples that he has made no concession to death. He is no ghost. His body is a real physical body. He eats and drinks (see also Acts 10:41).

This text is structured as follows:

Preface (vv. 1-2)
Timing: teaching about the Kingdom (vv. 3-8)
The ascension of Jesus (vv. 9-11)
Fulfilment of Scripture - Matthias replaces Judas (vv. 12-26)

(2) *Timing: teaching about the Kingdom (vv. 3-8)*

Between his resurrection and ascension there is a period of forty days (v. 3) in which Jesus continues to teach about the Kingdom of God. In verses 4-5, he tells the Eleven the point they have reached in the unfolding of God's purposes. They are not to go out into ministry immediately, but must wait for the baptism of the Holy Spirit, promised by God the Father (Luke 11:13).

Forty days after resurrection, ten days before Pentecost, the disciples ask a question which betrays a right expectation, but the wrong timing: 'Lord, are you at this time going to restore the Kingdom to Israel?' (v. 6) As resurrected Messiah, will Jesus now bring down the curtain of history, restore Israel to her rightful place and reign over all creation?

Jesus redirects their concern and makes it clear that before this happens there is more work to be done. It will not merely be human work, however, but Spirit-empowered witness. They are commanded to wait in Jerusalem (v. 4). They will receive power when the Spirit comes upon them (v. 8). This is the gift of which John the Baptist spoke (v. 5), and the effect of the Spirit's coming will be to empower the church in its witness. They are not to leave Jerusalem without having received the Holy Spirit. Ministry is a supernatural activity. The church is not merely a human institution, but a divinely-infused group of people.

(3) *The ascension of Jesus (vv. 9-11)*

Jesus is then 'taken up' (Luke 24:51; Acts 1:2, 9, 11). The disciple's original question (v. 6) can only be answered affirmatively after the ascension, because the ascension guarantees the return of Christ as Lord 'to restore all things' (3:21). Confirming the message of those who announced the resurrection (Luke 24:4), two men tell the disciples that just as he has been taken up, so he will certainly return (1:11). There is a limited time until his return, and there is work to be done.

The resurrection was the necessary preliminary to his ascension. It showed that death has no hold over Jesus, confirming that he is God's Anointed, the Messiah (2:31). The ascension then is the glorification or coronation of God the Son at the Father's right hand. At the completion of his work, Jesus Christ is restored by the Father to his rightful place. What Peter, John and James glimpsed in the transfiguration is now Christ's permanent state (Luke 9:28-36). He now rules, occupying the highest place, as Lord of all, from where he exercises his universal dominion (Acts 10:36, Phil 2:9). He will pour out his Holy Spirit, give gifts to his church (Eph. 4:11), and intercede for us (Rom. 8:34). Little wonder that we are urged to set our hearts and minds on things above, where Christ is seated at God's right hand (Col. 3:1-3)!

Christ's ascension to the right-hand of the Father made a deep impact on the apostles. They realised it was God's ultimate declaration of Jesus' Lordship. The ascension thus became the climactic point in apostolic preaching. When preaching in the temple at Pentecost, Peter declares Christ to be at God's right hand, and the apostles as witnesses to this fact (2:32-35). The gift of the Spirit is the indication that Jesus is where he said he would be (2:32; Luke 22:69). Peter solemnly exposes the terrible truth that Israel crucified the One God declared (by ascension) to be Lord. Peter promises that the ascended Lord will send the Holy Spirit on his hearers (2:38), just as Christ promised he would send the Spirit upon the apostles (1:5). After healing the lame beggar at the Beautiful Gate of the temple, Peter preaches Christ as the ascended King who will return to restore all things (3:21). It is Peter's insistence that Jesus is the ascended King, and that the apostles are witnesses of this, that enrages the Jewish Council in Jerusalem (5:31). Similarly, it was Stephen's declaration that he was seeing the ascended Christ that finally provoked his stoning (7:56).

Clearly, the ascension of Christ, declaring him to be Lord, and the significance of the apostles witnessing this event, was a truth of such importance that the apostles were willing to die for it. And so too were those like Stephen who joined them in their preaching ministries.

(4) Fulfilment of Scripture - Matthias replaces Judas (vv. 12-26)

When Jesus ascended the disciples numbered around a hundred and twenty (v. 15). After the crucifixion, their hopes were dashed. With the resurrection, their gloom was displaced by hope and joy. What will be their response to Christ's ascension? Will they return to hopeless despair because they are apart from their Lord again? It is something of a surprise to find the Christians going about their business as usual immediately after the ascension. They return to Jerusalem, where Jesus told them they were to wait for the gift of God (v. 4) and set themselves to pray earnestly (v. 14).

Peter seems to be the acknowledged leader and spokesman for the group. It is Peter who sees the betrayal of Christ by Judas, and the selection of a replacement from among the disciples, as a fulfilment of Psalms 69:25 and 109:8. To qualify for selection, a man must have been with the apostles from the time John was baptizing until the ascension of Jesus. His central task is to be a witness to the resurrection. Two men are proposed, prayer is offered for guidance, lots are cast and Matthias is added to the apostolic group. This is the last recorded instance in Scripture of a lot being cast to determine God's mind.

Why does Luke include this detail? Why not move straight from the ascension to Pentecost? After all, Matthias is not mentioned again in the book. Judas' betrayal was a major failure of leadership that needed to be acknowledged and rectified. Luke's concern to provide a full and orderly record, is a 'warts and all' coverage of the history of the church. He does not idealise the church. Later, he records the hypocrisy of Ananias and Sapphira (ch. 5), the bickering of the widows (ch. 6), Peter's reluctance to heed God's call (ch. 10), even Paul's impatience with John Mark (ch. 15). The saying is true: 'The best of men are men at best.' We are to recognise our own frailty, just as Luke shows the church facing up to the need to renew its leadership following the apostasy of one of the apostles. Their example sets an important marker for the church today – sin and failure need to be acknowledged and dealt with.

With the appointment of Matthias, once more the apostolate is complete, and ready to witness to the reality of Christ's resurrection (v. 22) and lead the church. The continuity with the Old Testament people of God, represented by the twelve tribes of Israel, is clear from the need to restore the group to twelve.

Christ's involvement with the election of Matthias is reassuring. It shows that Jesus is neither uninterested nor uninvolved in his church. He continues to lead and guide from heaven through His Spirit. Nothing is outside the scope of his control. Both Judas' betrayal and Matthias' election are in fulfilment of God's Word.

(5) Summary
Now that Jesus has ascended, will things be different? The answer is 'Yes' and 'No'! Yes, it will be different, for Jesus Christ will no longer be visibly with his church, but no, for Jesus Christ is still Lord of the church and he will continue to guide, direct, rebuke and encourage. Augustine comments: 'For He departed, and behold, He is here!' (Augustine, *Confessions* IV, 19).

From text to teaching
(1) Get the message clear
Big idea (theme)
Jesus Christ triumphantly ascends to the place of rule, from where he directs the church's choice of a replacement for Judas, and promises to pour out the Holy Spirit on his church.

Big question(s) (aim)
Preaching or teaching on this passage should answer the following questions:

+ What does the ascension mean for Jesus and us?
+ Where is Christ?
+ What does Christ in heaven continue to do on earth?

(2) Engage the hearer
Point of contact
'Yes and No' is a very Irish answer to a question! A friend of mine travelling on a bus in Dublin heard a man ask the

driver whether he knew where Foley Street was. 'Yes and No', replied the driver. 'No, I don't know where Foley Street is, but yes, I know a fellow who does!'

In response to the disciples (and our) question: 'Does the ascension of Jesus change his relationship with us?' Luke's answer is very Irish: 'Yes and No!'

Dominant picture(s)
The sight of Christ being taken up into the cloud is such a startling one that you would never forget it. Following the resurrection the disciples knew that they could expect anything. The resurrection changes gloom into hope and surprising joy. Will the ascension turn the hope back into gloom?

(3) *Work on application*
Necessary application(s)
No matter how urgent the task, the disciples were not to begin their ministry without the Holy Spirit. In all that the church does, it is to do it in the power of the Spirit.

Christ chose the apostles while he was on earth (v. 2) and after his ascension, he continued to choose from heaven (v. 24). Divine guidance was given through drawing lots. This is the last mention in Scripture of a lot being cast to determine God's will. We continue to be guided by the Spirit, but through the Spirit-inspired Word, conveyed to us by the Apostles whose number was completed by the Spirit's choice after the ascension, and whose ability to faithfully proclaim God's plan was enabled by the Spirit's power. The pattern for the church is thus one of prayerfulness, seeking the ascended Lord's guidance, while paying heed to the teaching of his appointed apostles.

The church is the only institution on earth that is not merely human. The Son of God directs his church from heaven. The church must recognize its unique role, invest its confidence in the Lord to guide and direct it, and believe that God will ultimately fulfil his purposes through it.

Refute impossible application(s)

An impossible application is to hold to a man-centered view of the world; that we have a purely human charter, with only human and material resources available to us. The ascended Christ reigns and rules from heaven. We are not free to live and serve independently. We need the resources provided by God's Spirit.

An impossible application is that Christ is uninterested in his cause on earth. His Spirit-directed activity of guiding his church from heaven shows that he is neither remote nor uninvolved.

An impossible application is that active planning, strategising, wise application of good business principles (while all useful), are sufficient for discernment and growth in the church. Prayer to the ascended Christ is essential. A desire to engage in ministry activity must not crowd out prayer. Jesus is responsive to our prayers.

Possible application(s)

Do I reflect enough on the fact that Jesus has overcome and is at the Father's side? Do I recognise that he is ruler over all that happens in the world?

Do I see trusting prayer as the first response to serving God as his people in the world? Am I vigilant, lest prayer be displaced by activity in the church?

Proclaiming the message

A preaching outline

Title: 'Will things be different? Yes and No!'

Text: **Acts 1:1-26**

(1) 'Yes and No' - a good 'Irish' response to a question!
- A remarkable sight (v. 9)
- A good question (v. 6)
- A realistic answer (vv. 7-8)

(2) Yes, things will be different (vv. 9-11)

(3) No, things will not be different (vv. 12-26)
- *What we must not do*
  Think of ministry, church or of ourselves in merely human ways apart from the 'the gift of the Father'.
- *What we may do…*
  Focus more on Christ's role, his dominion, his direction of his church, the church as his body.
- *What we must do…*
  Move out in prayerful dependence on Christ.

Leading a Bible study

Title: 'Will things be different? Yes and No!'

Text: **Acts 1:1-26**

(1) Introduce the issues

Nobody likes change, especially if the change involves the loss of a particularly supportive friendship. How do you think the disciples felt as they negotiated the roller coaster of emotion involved in seeing Jesus die, then rise and now being told he is to be taken back to heaven?

(2) *Study the passage*
Acts 1:1-26

i)   How similar is the introduction in Acts 1:1-2 to the introduction in Luke 1:1-4?

ii) What is the disciples' concern and how does Jesus' response provide a corrective to them (vv. 6-8)?

iii) Verses 9-11 record the ascension. Identify the parallels to the resurrection in Luke 24:1-8. What is the promise given by the two men at the tomb?

iv) How does Peter understand Judas' betrayal of Jesus? Why does there need to be a replacement (vv. 12-21)?

v)   How does the choice of Matthias in verses 24-26 show that even though Jesus is ascended he is still in control?

vii) Verse 26 is the last time a lot is cast in the New Testament. Why is that so?

(3) *Think it through*

i)   Why is the ascension of Jesus important for him and for us?

ii) What is Jesus' ministry in heaven now?

(4) *Live it out*

i)   Jesus makes it clear that ministry can only be effective through the Holy Spirit. And therefore the disciples had to wait for the Holy Spirit before beginning their ministry. In verse 5 they are told not to leave Jerusalem until they receive the 'gift my Father promised', are 'baptised with the Holy Spirit', and 'receive power when the Holy Spirit comes on you' (vv. 4, 5, 8). What does this teach us about our own need to have the Holy Spirit fill us for ministry?

ii)   Are you aware of your dependence on the Spirit?

iii) Are you confident in the power of the Spirit within you for powerful witness?

How does the ascension of Christ encourage you?

5

'How To Be Fully And Forever Equipped'

(Acts 2:1-13; 8:14-17)

Listening to the text
(1) Setting: the day of Pentecost

Pentecost, one of the three main festivals of Judaism (the other two being Passover and Tabernacles), was ten days after Christ's ascension. In the Greek, *pente-* is the root for fifty; the festival of Pentecost was so named because it occurred fifty days after Passover. Originally, Pentecost celebrated the conclusion of the barley harvest. The first cuttings of the harvest were kept, made into bread and offered at the completion of the harvest (Lev. 23:15-17). As time went on, Pentecost came to commemorate the giving of the law to Moses on Sinai, following the Passover when the redemption of the people from Egypt was remembered. The Pentecost Festival, therefore, was all about fulfilment, completion and finality. The completion of Christ's work was marked by the pouring out of his Spirit (Acts 2:33) and birth of his body, the church. It is fitting that this great fulfilment should occur at Pentecost.

Pentecost then is the beginning of the end; the Holy Spirit a foretaste of the new age, a down payment on the inheritance which is ours and for which we groan in anticipation (Rom. 8:23; Eph. 1:13-14)

(2) *What was seen and heard*
(i) *The sound and sight (vv. 2-3)*
The coming of the Spirit is associated with the sound of wind and the sight of fire. In John 3:8, Jesus speaks explicitly of the Spirit and the wind. When God visited Moses in the theophany of Exodus 3:2, flames of fire were present. God used a strong east wind to blow back the Red Sea, and in a pillar of fire he led the people of God out of Egypt, to Sinai, and then to the Promised Land. The combination of the sound of a violent wind and tongues of flame resting on each of the one hundred and twenty was the indication of a visitation from God. What Jesus told them to wait for, and what John the Baptist said the Christ would do, was now happening. They were being baptized with the Holy Spirit and with fire (Luke 3:16).

The difference between this theophany and Old Testament occurrences is instructive. God's Spirit is not just present with his people corporately, leading them collectively; rather, each *individual* believer gathered that day in Jerusalem is touched by fire. Both men and woman receive the Spirit, as do apostles and ordinary believers. One writer describes Pentecost as 'the democratization of the Spirit'.

(ii) *Other tongues (vv. 4-13)*
The one hundred and twenty were filled with the Spirit, enabling them to speak in 'other tongues'. The Greek word is *glossa* (speaking in tongues is thus referred to as *glossolalia*).

In Jerusalem at the time were Jewish pilgrims from the fifteen different areas listed in verses 9-11. It is estimated that the population of Jerusalem, normally around fifty-five thousand in the first century, could increase dramatically at festival time to two hundred thousand, or more. Here were Jews from fifteen different language groups hearing among the utterances of the hundred and twenty the wonders of God being declared in their own mother tongues (v. 11). Again the word is *glossa*.

This event is quite different from what is typically labelled as tongues-speaking in Christian gatherings today. Very often, so-called tongues-speaking is unformed, unintelligible language.

Verse 6 makes it clear that this is not just a miracle of hearing, but truly a miracle of speaking. This tongues-speaking was the Holy Spirit enabling each of the hundred and twenty to speak a language without having learned that language. The word used in verse 6 for language, synonymous with tongue in verse 4 and verse 11, is the word 'dialect' - a definite, discernible language.

When Cornelius and his friends are baptised in the Holy Spirit, they too speak in tongues and Peter and the witnesses understand them to be magnifying God. They understood this to be a duplicate of their own experience (10:46-47). I take that to mean that they too spoke in formal, formed language.

Vivid writer as he is, Luke describes the crowd's reactions:

+ bewilderment - literally, stopped in their tracks (v. 6);
+ utterly amazed - literally, swept off their feet (v. 7);
+ amazed and perplexed; they find it incredible, inexplicable (v. 12);
+ some mocked, 'they must be drunk' (v. 13).

This sort of mixed reaction is a typical response to God's work throughout Acts.

(3) Dominant themes
(i) The coming of the Holy Spirit

The coming of the Spirit on God's people, as a permanent resident in their lives, is spoken of by Jeremiah 31:33 and Ezekiel 36:25-27. Peter sees the Pentecost event as fulfilling Joel 2:28-32. Earlier, Luke refers to Elizabeth and Zechariah being filled with the Holy Spirit (Luke 1:41, 67) but these were temporary and particular fillings. Now the Holy Spirit comes to reside permanently, animating the body of Christ (Eph. 3:16-19). Here then is the wonder of the gospel: an assured relationship with God, of life and blessing, rather than judgment and curse because of the forgiveness of sins secured for us by Christ, and a dynamic relationship with God whereby Christ dwells within us in the person of his Spirit (Col. 1:27).

This baptism of the Holy Spirit is a once and for all baptism, but Luke mentions many fillings of the Spirit (e.g. 4:8, 31; 13:9). Since the first century, this has given rise to a good deal of confusing and sometimes disturbing teaching in Christian circles. In particular, there has been much divergent teaching about how we receive the baptism of the Holy Spirit.

When I was a new believer I was taught that this baptism would come at some time after conversion, and would be evidenced by the manifestation of a strange tongue. This conclusion was usually arrived at by extrapolating from the experience of the Samaritan believers in Acts 8:14-17. The Samaritans first heard the gospel through Philip, who left Jerusalem due to the persecution that broke out after

Stephen's stoning. Their Christian experience, according to 8:12, was that they heard the gospel, believed and were baptised, but they did not receive the Holy Spirit. Verse 16 is an amazing verse - what does Luke mean when he says that the Samaritans had simply been baptized into the name of the Lord Jesus? Should they have been baptized in the name of the Father, and of the Son and of the Holy Spirit? Regardless of whatever inadequacies there were in the teaching they received, Peter and John came from Jerusalem, prayed for them, and placed their hands on them. Subsequent to their conversion they receive the Holy Spirit.

This raises the obvious question: is this to be the normal pattern of Christian experience? In order to give an assured answer, we need to stand back from this particular text and ask an important question about Acts overall. The question is this: if Luke's purpose is to show a *normal* pattern of experience, why doesn't he show us a *consistent* pattern? There are so many different experiences in Acts, it is difficult to opt for just one and say it is normative, and others not. Having the big picture will help us here. There may be background to an event that accounts for the particular details Luke records. In this instance, there is an obvious historical, political and religious background. There was a long-standing division between Judea and Samaria. God, by delaying the Samaritans' reception of the Spirit, acknowledges this division, but also ends it. The Jew/Samaritan division is not to be tolerated in the church; in other words, there is not to be a Jewish church and a Samaritan church. The Jewish church in Jerusalem had to recognise that just as God had saved them, so he makes no distinction, saving the Samaritans in the same way. The visit of Peter and John would ensure the breaking down of this barrier. The Samaritans would receive the Spirit from the Jerusalem church-leaders' hands, and Peter and John would tell their brothers of the integrity of the Samaritan experience. And the Samaritans would recognise that they had received the Spirit at the hand of the Jerusalem apostles. Therefore, there would be no justification for continuing the barrier between the Samaritan and the Jerusalem church. Since the apostles believed *before* Christ had ascended and poured out the Spirit, they could not receive the Spirit at the time of believing. Therefore, their circumstances were unique and should not be treated as normative for those who believe after Pentecost.

However, it is clear that our experience today should not be the experience of the hundred and twenty, or of the first Samaritan believers, but of the three thousand in Jerusalem (v. 41) who repented, were baptized and received the forgiveness of their sins and the gift of the Holy Spirit (v. 38). No description is given of external phenomena accompanying their reception of the Spirit. If they occurred and were important for us to know about, Luke would have recorded them.

It is important that we point out the dangers of teaching a second tier, extra experience of the Holy Spirit beyond conversion to Christ, thereby erecting a barrier within the body of Christ that falsely demarcates those who have had the deeper experience, from those who have not. Equally, however, we must beware of throwing the baby out with the bathwater. In our reformed circles, we need more awareness of the indwelling Spirit and more confidence in him to do his work.

(ii) The filling of the Holy Spirit
Paul exhorts the Ephesians in 5:18 to go on continually being filled with the Spirit by speaking, singing, giving thanks and submitting. Ordinary, every day activities for Christians, yet these activities are the way to maintain the fullness of the Spirit within.

(iii) The significance of Pentecost
The Holy Spirit has come upon the church and he enables effective witness. He is the empowering Spirit!

Matthew Henry comments that the significance of the Pentecost event is to dignify and so to distinguish these men as messengers from heaven, so that like Moses at the bush, 'the crowd will turn aside and see this great sight!' (Matthew Henry, *Commentary on the Whole Bible*, Vol vi, p. 18).

From text to teaching
(1) Get the message clear
Big idea (theme)
The Holy Spirit comes upon the church, enabling those whom he baptizes to speak miraculously in languages they had not learned.

Big question(s) (aim)
Preaching or teaching on this passage should answer the following questions:

  ✦   How do we receive the Holy Spirit?
  ✦   Why do we need the Holy Spirit?
  ✦   How can I be fully equipped for life and ministry?

(2) Engage the hearer
Point of contact

Most people will have had experience of the pleasant familiarity of their mother tongue when visiting a foreign city. William Cameron Townsend, founder of Wycliffe Bible Translators, makes a powerful point: 'The greatest missionary is the Bible in the mother tongue. It never needs a furlough and never is considered a foreigner' ('*The Smoke of a Thousand Villages*' *and other stories of real live heroes of the faith*, p. 110). These two insights can be used as a bridge into the tongues speaking event at Pentecost.

Dominant picture(s)

The response of the crowd show what an overwhelming event this is. Wind, fire, and the wonders of God being described in each hearer's mother tongue - these are awesome signs, signalling the approach of God. Think about your own experience of awesome signs signalling the approach of some great event.

(3) Work on application
Necessary application(s)

Rejoice in the fullness of the complete Christian experience, forgiveness of sin, divine empowerment for life and witness from the indwelling Holy Spirit. You are a supernaturally enabled person. What happened to the hundred and twenty over two stages and to the three thousand in one stage, is also our experience.

Refute impossible application(s)

The following impossible applications might helpfully be stated and refuted:

+ Christianity is one worldview, philosophical system, works-centred religion, like any other. At its heart, it's about humans trying harder to please God: 'God helps those who help themselves'.
+ Pastors need better management techniques more than anything else.

Possible application(s)
+ Am I consciously aware of the Holy Spirit living within?
+ Do I show enough confidence in the Spirit to do his work?
+ Do I live in the reality of being a supernaturally empowered person at home, at work and in church?

Proclaiming the message
A preaching outline
Title: 'How To Be Fully And Forever Equipped'
Texts: Acts 2:1-13; 8:14-17

Introduction: the mother tongue
(1) The birthday of the church?
+ the Day (v. 1)
+ the sound and sight (vv. 2-3)
+ the tongues (v. 4)
+ the miracle (v. 6)
+ the crowd (vv. 6, 7, 12-13)

(2) **How are we to receive the baptism (Acts 8:14-17)?**

(3) **Come to Jesus, the baptizer** (John 7:37-39)

Leading a Bible study
Title: **'How To Be Fully And Forever Equipped'**
Text: **Acts 2:1-13; 8:14-17**

(1) Introduce the issues
The apostles and disciples who had been with Jesus and were eye witnesses of his death and resurrection were told to wait until they had been equipped with the Holy Spirit. If *they* needed him for *their* ministry, how much more do we need him today?

(2) Study the passages
Acts 2:1-13; 8:14-17

i)   Why is it significant that God should pour out his Spirit on the day of Pentecost?

ii)   The disciples began to speak in tongues (v. 4), languages (v. 6), tongues (v. 11). What was this miracle?

iii)   How many language groups were represented at Jerusalem? What was the response of the crowd?

iv)   In Acts 8:14-17, the Samaritan believers receive the Holy Spirit. If they had believed, why hadn't they received the Holy Spirit when they believed?

v)   How would you refute the argument that both the disciples of chapter 2 and Samaritans of chapter 8 receive the Spirit as a post-conversion experience, and therefore, so should we?

vi)   Do you think the book of Acts shows us how the believer today is to receive the Spirit (see also Acts 10:44-46 and 19:1-7)?

vii)   How should we receive the Holy Spirit (see John 7:37-39; Rom. 8:9; Eph. 1:13-14)?

(3) *Think it through*

i) In Acts 2:38, Peter says that forgiveness of sin and the gift of the Holy Spirit are God's provision for the believers' past and present. How important is it for us to know the Holy Spirit equipping us for powerful witness?

ii) Christianity is a relationship. Are you aware of a conscious relationship with God, the Father, the Son and the Holy Spirit?

(4) *Live it out*

i) In your daily life of witness, how do you show confidence in the Holy Spirit to do his work of being your co-witness?

ii) See John 15:26-27: 'Your witness is part of a twofold, effective ministry:'...he will testify... you also must testify...' In what ways are you aware of the Holy Spirit prompting you to speak the gospel and empowering your testimony so that it is powerful?

iii) Unseen does not mean unreal. How do you think we accept the lie of the world that the unseen, the Spirit, is unreal?

iv) Why is the truth of the Spirit residing in us so incredible (see Col. 1:27)?

6
'It's All About Jesus'

(Acts 2:14-47)

Listening to the text

In Acts, crowds and preaching go together like a horse and carriage. Here Peter is the preacher; the crowd, the one that witnessed the miracle of Pentecost. Peter, who had previously denied Jesus, now proclaims him. First, he deals with the response of mockery, that the disciples were drunk (vv. 13, 15). 'They are not', he says, 'It's too early in the morning.' Then he interprets the event. Since he is preaching to a Jewish audience, the speech is peppered with Old Testament quotations. His point: this event is a fulfilment of those Scriptures.

(1) Important details

Verses 17-21 are a quote from Joel 2:28-32. Verse 18: '...and they will prophecy' (that is, they will 'interpret Scriptural truth') is Peter's addition to the original text from Joel. Peter thereby affirms that these are the last days, when God's Spirit will come on all his people of all ages and sexes, even his servants. These days will be marked by wonders in the created order. Salvation will be offered freely to all who call on the Lord.

Peter then shows that the event is all about Jesus (v. 14). We might expect him to preach on the Spirit, but as elsewhere, the focus is the Lord Jesus (see Acts 19:1-6, where an ignorance of the Spirit is met by an explanation of Jesus' person and work). Peter affirms the following about Jesus:

+ He was accredited by God through miracles, signs and wonders (v. 22).

+ He was handed over to you, and with the help of wicked men, you nailed him to the cross. But this was the fulfilment of God's purposes (v. 23).

+ There was a clear and stark contrast between what you did, and what God did. You put him to death, but it was impossible for death to keep its hold on him (v. 24).

+ Psalm 16:8-11: 'You will not abandon me to the grave, nor let your holy one see decay' (quoted in Acts 2:27). Prophetically, David spoke of the resurrection of Christ, that he was not abandoned to the grave (v. 31).

+ The apostles are eye-witnesses of the resurrection of Jesus (v. 32).

+ Jesus is now exalted to the right hand of God. The pouring out of the Holy Spirit is proof that He is there.

+ Again, David was not speaking of himself when he wrote Psalm 110:1, but of Jesus (vv. 34-35).

+ God has made Jesus both Lord and Christ (v. 36). The Septuagint translates Yahweh's name as Kurios; here we are told that Yahweh has made Jesus Kurios and the Christ, the long awaited Messiah. Therefore Jesus is the incarnation of Yahweh.

Peter's boldness is notable. He draws the clearest contrast between what they did and what God did (vv. 23-24). He shows how their Scriptures can only be understood in the light of Jesus Christ, the interpretive key. The crowd is deeply convicted by Peter's speech (v. 37). Luke describes their reaction as 'cut to the heart'. It conveys the idea of piercing, showing the powerful nature of the message (Heb. 4:12). The word has similar meaning to the one used of the response of the Sanhedrin in 5:33 and 7:54, although there the idea has more to do with 'cut', associated with anger. In response to their deep conviction, Peter boldly calls on them to repent of their opposition to Jesus, and be baptized as the external sign of this inner repentance. Then they will be forgiven and receive the Holy Spirit.

(2) Dominant themes
(i) Salvation
Here then is the description of the salvation of Acts 2:21 and 2:40. It involves both take and give. God takes and deals with sin and gives his Holy Spirit. The one deals with our past, the other ensures new life now, and in the future. Three thousand were saved that day (2:41).

(ii) The Church
Luke follows with a description (2:42-47) of the community life of the prototype church. They shared the common experience of hearing the gospel, repentance and baptism, and now they shared a common devotion

(the word carries the sense of 'attachment like glue'). They stuck to the apostolic teaching and to the community and the breaking of bread (the 'breaking of bread' may indicate the Lord's Supper or, as in verse 46, hospitality and prayer).

In John 17:23, Jesus had prayed for the complete unity of believers. We now see this deep unity built around a common experience and common devotion. This even extended to a Spirit-motivated voluntary socialism (vv. 44-45). We may think that the church was fairly self-absorbed, but no, their pooling of resources was to meet human need. At a time when government was not concerned for social welfare and life was cut-throat and cheap, no wonder people were impressed with this new society growing up in their midst in Jerusalem 'enjoying the favour of all the people' (v. 47).

Again Luke reminds us that this impressive community is not just a matter of people turning over a new leaf, but a radical transformation superintended by God (v. 43). God enabled the apostles to do wonders and 'the Lord added to their number' (v. 47). This is God at work through the life and witness of his people.

The church is never to be a closed, secret and introverted community. All true fellowship is founded upon and focused on the gospel. All true fellowship overflows into evangelism, which, after all, is the overarching mandate of the church (Acts 1:8)

You need such a fellowship with your fellow believers. The fractured world needs to see church communities witnessing to the reality of gospel wrought restored human relationships.

From text to teaching

(1) Get the message clear

Big idea (theme)

Jesus is God's Messiah: crucified, raised, ascended. From heaven He has poured out the Holy Spirit. Through repentance towards this Jesus, we are set right with God and join the Spirit-filled, new covenant community.

Big question(s) (aim)

Preaching or teaching on this passage should answer the following questions:

+ How do I receive forgiveness and the Holy Spirit?
+ Who is the Holy Spirit, where does He come from, and what does He do?
+ What should the church be like?

(2) Engage the hearer

Point of contact

There are a number of potential 'contact points' for teaching from this section of Acts.

Here are two:

Is Pentecost about the Spirit?

It would be logical to expect preaching on the Spirit at Pentecost. So it may come as something of a surprise that at the first Pentecost, the preaching was all about Jesus. The mismatch between our expectation and biblical reality, very often reveals an area where we need to grow in our understanding. Are we willing to have our preconceptions challenged by Scripture? This can be particularly difficult when our hearers consider themselves to be living in 'spiritually sensitive' days. People today tend to be more fascinated with a Holy Spirit than with the historic Jesus. But to preach Jesus is to preach the focus of the Spirit.

Do you seek rest and happiness?
Note the words of this anonymous hymn:

'I sighed for rest and happiness,
I yearned for them, not thee,
but while I passed my Saviour by,
his love laid hold of me.
Now none but Christ can satisfy.'

To seek the rest and happiness of the hymn is similar to seeking the Spirit. All are found through their source: a relationship with the Lord Jesus. The presence of the Spirit, the fruit of the Spirit, Christian community; none are possible without the root - Jesus Christ and faith in him.

Dominant picture(s)
A number of the teaching strands in this passage lend themselves to visualisation, provoking powerful emotive responses:

- Humans do their worst, but God uses it for his best – like Joseph's experience (Gen. 50:20).
- The Holy Spirit did not come from nowhere. The Father gives Him to the ascended Son, who gives Him to His people.
- The Son is exalted; his enemies are his footstool.

+ The church displays a visible and tangible unity:'devotion', 'all', 'together', 'everyone', 'common' are the words used.

(3) Work on application
Necessary application(s)
Repentance to Christ is the only way to receive forgiveness and the Holy Spirit, and to become members of the Christian community. Repentance involves turning from any conviction about Jesus, other than that He was crucified, raised, ascended, and now reigns as Lord and Christ.

Refute impossible application(s)
The following impossible applications might helpfully be stated and refuted:

+ The events and preaching at Pentecost make it clear that the fruit of salvation, the Spirit, and forgiveness are not available apart from relationship with Jesus Christ. The impossible application is that they are!
+ It will not do to say that the Christian life is just a matter of trying hard to live a moral life, or simply a matter of 'loving God' with no conviction about Jesus. What we make of Christ will determine what God makes of us.
+ The events of Pentecost, and the subsequent activity of the Christian community that formed in Jerusalem after Pentecost, show that the church is not merely a human institution. It cannot be analysed properly in merely human categories – whether psychological, sociological or managerial. The Spirit of God is present in his church.

Possible application(s)
The Christian life is one of repentance and faith. I need to realise in an ongoing way that I am not Lord, and that Jesus only is Lord. Repentance is that recognition, turning away from my own lordship and recognising his Lordship. Is this necessary recognition of his Lordship part of my everyday Christian walk?

Proclaiming the message
A preaching outline
Title: 'It's All About Jesus'
Text: Acts 2:14-47

(1)   **Joel and Pentecost** (vv. 17-21)
(2)   **The Psalms and Jesus** (vv. 22-36)
(3)   **The crowd's response** (vv. 37-41)
(4)   **Prototype Church** (vv. 42-47)

Leading a Bible study
Title: 'It's All About Jesus'
Text: Acts 2:14-47

(1) Introduce the issues
i)   Peter's preaching focuses on Jesus and not, as we might expect at Pentecost, on the Holy Spirit.
ii)   The Spirit-filled community is marked by open-handed sharing of food, possessions and of all that they have in Christ.
iii)   Such an attractive fellowship is irresistible to the world.

(2) *Study the passage*

Acts 2:14-47

i)   Peter refutes the mockery of verse 13 and asserts Pentecost is a fulfilment of Joel (Acts 2:16-21). How does Pentecost fulfil Joel?

ii) Why does Peter quote David in Acts 2:25-28 (Psalm 16:8-11) and Acts 2:34-35 (Ps. 110:1)?

iii) In 2:22-36, what does Peter assert about Jesus? Why was it impossible for death to keep its grip on Jesus (v. 24)?

iv) How does Peter contrast Israel's treatment of Jesus with God's treatment of Jesus?

v)   What is the response of the crowd and what does Peter tell them to do (vv. 37-39)?

vi) Explain verse 39. How is the promise to 'your children and for all who are far off'?

vii) How would you describe the atmosphere of Peter's address? Why do you think Luke gives these statistical summaries at 2:41, 47; 4:4; 6:7; 9:31; 16:5?

viii) How would you describe the life of the prototype church (vv. 42-47)?

ix) Why did the church enjoy the favour of the people (v. 47)?

(3) *Think it through*

i)   How closely does the message of the church today follow the message of Peter?

ii) How clearly do our churches model the life of the early church community?

iii) How does Peter show the empowering witness of the Spirit in his preaching?

(4) Live it out

i)   The coming of the Spirit is the proof that Jesus is at
     the Father's right hand (v. 33). Jesus lives and continues
     to pour out his Spirit on all who repent and believe.
     The early church's devotions reflect a vivid awareness
     of these truths (v. 42). How does our community
     compare?

ii) What can we do to bring about change in our church
     so that it is far more like the prototype?

iii) Do you think that such a description in verses 42-47
     could be realistic for our community life in the twenty-
     first century?

7

'THE TRIUMPHANT INDICATIVE'

(ACTS 3)

Listening to the text
(1) Setting
According to Acts 2:43 and 5:12, the apostles performed many miraculous signs and wonders. This chapter records just one of them. It falls into two sections: the sign (3:1-10), and the sermon (3:11-26).

Moreover, the setting is purposely ironic. At the outset of his dynamic book Luke presents us with a number of ironies. Not least of these is the fact that Acts begins with a miracle concerning a totally immobile man, yet goes on to recount how the gospel progresses from Jerusalem to Rome, and is very mobile indeed! Beside the temple gate, called 'Beautiful' (v. 2), a congenital cripple begging for alms is a pitiable sight. This man is reduced to begging outside the temple of God's old covenant people. The old covenant community had degenerated to such an extent that they had overlooked their obligations (Deut. 15:4, 7-8). This is a clear contrast with the new covenant community, selling property to ensure the needs of all their members were met (Acts 2:45 and 4:32-37).

(2) *The Sign (3:1-10)*
(i) *Jesus' Action through the Apostle*
The helplessness of the man is stressed. He had to be carried every day to beg at the gate. Peter and John go to the temple at 3pm., the other hours of prayer being 9am. and 12pm. God so arranged that Peter and John had no coins to share with him, but Peter is clear regarding God's intention. He speaks as Christ's representative, telling the man to walk (v. 6). What Jesus alone had previously done (Luke 5:22-26) Peter now does in his name, as his representative.

The response is outstanding. It's not that he gradually grew stronger, but instantaneously his feet and ankles became strong so that he walked and jumped, all the time praising God (vv. 7-8). This miracle involved the healing of the body, the creation of previously non-existent muscle tissue. The brain then had to be taught to use and direct limbs to do what they had never done before. And the man was over forty years of age (4:22)! This is a remarkable sign of creative restoration (4:16). Even if the healing were possible today, years of therapy would be involved to fully restore the man. The fact of his healing is stressed by Luke's repeated references to him walking, three times in verses 7-9.

It is clear that just as God had accredited Jesus by signs and wonders (Acts 2:22), so now the apostles were being accredited. Fresh periods of revelation in Scripture are accompanied by such signs in order to attest to the integrity of what is being said (Heb. 2:4). It is clear that it is not merely human power at work in this healing. Jesus Christ is the source of such a sign (see Acts 4:10). Its manifestation is the indication of Christ's approval of his messengers, and what they are about to declare.

The apostolic gospel preached in Acts needs no new approval from God today - it already has his attestation. The historically validated healing of this man was God's accreditation of this gospel then, and it remains God's accreditation today.

(ii) A sign to preach!
Once again, in vivid terms, Luke records the reaction of the crowd, as he had at Pentecost (v. 10). The gathering of a crowd in Acts is always seen as an opportunity for preaching. The Spirit empowers boldness and such boldness consists of clarity and directness, but here we see that it is also opportunistic. Peter doesn't wait to be invited to speak; he takes the opportunity: 'When Peter saw this he said to them...' (v. 12). There is no doubt in the apostle's mind that the church is mandated to preach. The sign draws the crowd and accredits the message.

Peter, the main source of material which Mark used in his gospel, would have remembered Jesus' words recorded in Mark 1:38 when the disciples and the crowd were looking for him to heal. Jesus affirmed that he had come to preach: 'That is why I have come'. The healing of the paralysed beggar was a means of solving his even deeper need, as well as the deeper need of the crowd for spiritual and eternal health. And so Peter preaches to them.

What a sight it must have been! They heard Peter and they saw the man standing next to them (v. 11). First century medicine could have done nothing for him. Indeed, twenty-first century medicine could do nothing for him. So how did he come to be restored? Those most humanly responsible for the healing tell the crowd it has nothing to do with their power.

(3) *The Sermon (3:11-26)*
Not only is the sermon opportunistic, it is immediately self-effacing. Peter begins by deflecting attention from himself and John (v. 12), just as Barnabas and Paul were to do in Lystra (14:14ff). Peter's immediate concern is to give the glory to God, and directs his hearers to do likewise by repentance. Here is an outline of his sermon:

+ The God of the patriarchs, Abraham, Isaac and Jacob, has glorified his servant Jesus (v. 13). There is the clearest contrast between what you, his people, did to his servant and what God did to him. You 'handed him over', 'disowned' and 'killed' him. You did this to God's servant, 'the Holy and Righteous One', 'the author of life'. But God 'glorified' him (v. 13) and 'raised him from the dead' (v. 15).

+ We apostles are witnesses of this death and resurrection (v. 15). (Peter and the other apostles never forgot this commission (see Luke 24:48-49; Acts 1:22)).

+ This complete healing has come from Jesus. It is faith that comes from Jesus that is the conduit of this outstanding sign (v. 16).

+ God has exercised oversight of these events in order to fulfil his prophetic word. He has glorified Jesus despite your best efforts to destroy him (vv. 13, 18).

+ Repent (v. 19 (the same word as in 2:38)) in order to receive forgiveness of your sins and refreshment, while you wait for the Messianic age (vv. 20-21).

+ Jesus is the prophet like Moses, whom Moses said would come (Deut. 18:15-19). Like Moses, Jesus was from among your own, and God put his words in Jesus' mouth. And therefore, all disobedience of Jesus' words will be called to account.

+ These days are days of fulfilment of God's promise to Abraham (Gen. 12:3), to bless all peoples. You have the first opportunity of turning to Christ and showing the way for all peoples (vv. 22-26).

Because Peter's words are spoken to a Jewish audience, there are three direct references to the Old Testament (in vv. 22, 24, 25). As at Pentecost, there is a strong stress on fulfilment.

The crippled beggar did not heal himself. His healing is further accreditation of Jesus by God, accreditation of the apostles as his messengers, and accreditation of the apostolic gospel as his message. It shows that though Jesus has ascended, he is still active through his church. It is little wonder that Israel should repent of her disobedience and mistreatment of the Christ, as should we.

(4) Dominant themes
(i) The preacher's modus operandi - the triumphant indicative
J. Gresham Machen said that 'Christianity begins with the triumphant indicative'. Only when we have heard what God has done, can we rightly consider what we should do. The apostolic sermons in Acts are good examples of the indicative preceding the imperative.

The indicative mood of the verb is used to state facts. Here in Acts 3, indicatives describe God as glorifying and raising Jesus, in contrast to the Jews disowning and killing him (also indicatives). Indicatives are spread throughout

Peter's sermon in Acts 2 until he comes to verse 38, when
he calls on his hearers to 'repent and be baptised' - verbs
in the imperative mood. In Acts 3, the first imperative of
the sermon is in verse 19; showing the same order of the
imperative following the indicative.

All religion - Judaism, Hinduism, Islam, Buddhism, or
any other – focuses on people's effort to win and keep God's
favour. They always begin with the imperative - what people
must do. This is an indication that religion is actually an
expression of human rebellion against God. Religion is far
too optimistic about the human condition, because it calls
on people to do what we are incapable of doing. Biblical
Christianity alone begins with the proclamation of what
God has done – 'the triumphant indicative' – and only then
points out the appropriate human response of repentance
and faith (Acts 20:21).

Apostolic preaching always begins with an announce-
ment, a declaration of God's acts in history. This is God's
gospel (momentous news): the substitutionary death,
bodily resurrection, and triumphant ascension of his Lord
and Christ.

Today, as then, exhortation without exposition is powerless. To put it another way, imperative not preceded by indicative is powerless, because it depends upon people doing what
they are unable to do. It is the proclamation of the indicative,
then and now, which makes the imperative possible.

(ii) The preacher's expectation – a divided response from hearers
Another pattern of Acts is about to be seen, that of the
divided response of the hearers to the gospel. Acts 4:1-4
is the record of the hostile response of the Jewish religious
authorities. Yet in clear contrast, despite their hostility, God

continues to build his people. By verse 4, the church now numbers five thousand men. Opposition to Christ now becomes opposition to his apostles and his people.

From text to teaching

(1) Get the message clear
Big idea (theme)

The main thrust of Acts 3 is clear: through the healing of a crippled man, God continues to accredit Jesus as the ascended Christ, the apostles as his representatives, and the apostolic message as his gospel.

Big question(s)(aim)

Preaching or teaching on this passage should answer the following questions:

+ How do we know the Christian gospel is true?
+ How can doubt about the Christian message be dispelled?
+ Why does God heal?
+ What is God's accredited gospel?
+ What should people do in response to what God has done?

(2) Engage the hearer
Point of contact

The contact point could again be Christian preconceptions about signs and miracles. Many miracles in Acts are referred to by people as signs (2:22, 43; 5:12; 6:8; 14:3; 15:12). But this miracle is the only one specifically called a sign by Luke. What is the significance of this?

John attaches signs to 'I am' statements; but here the sign is attached as God's guarantee or verification of the message.

The sign (3:1-10) is like the manufacturer's guarantee or warranty confirming the veracity of the message (3:11-26).

Dominant picture
The central event of the chapter presents us with an outstanding sign. Congenital paralysis is transformed to walking, jumping and praising God.

(3) Work on application
Necessary application(s)
The apostolic gospel, God's gospel, commands all people to repent in the light of God's triumphant indicatives.

Refute impossible application(s)
In the light of Peter's sermon, the Christian gospel cannot be considered as just one among many humanly inspired messages. We cannot allow statements such as 'God is one and all religions represent equally valid paths to him' to go unchallenged, no matter how much opposition such 'exclusivism' may generate. Acts 3 shows us that hostility to the exclusive claims of Christ is to be expected. How do you account for the healing of this man when those most closely involved insist that God did it?

Possible application(s)
The indicatives of this passage present a challenge to our view of ourselves as people who confess Christ as Lord:
+ Is my boldness marked by apostolic opportunism?
+ Do I recognise that today's gospel is a God-verified and accredited message?
+ Do I share the fresh expectation of Messiah's return when the full number of the elect are called?

+ Do I recognise that the identity of the people of God is marked by their listening to Jesus, God's prophet like Moses?

These indicatives provide an encouragement for us to act upon the imperatives that follow them:
+ Will we boldly proclaim the completed work of Christ and call people to repent?
+ Will we proclaim Christianity as 'done', in contrast to the call of all other religions upon people to 'do'?

Proclaiming the message
A preaching outline
Title: 'The Triumphant Indicative'
Text: Acts 3

The gospel and doubt
(1) The sign (vv. 1-10)
(2) The sermon (vv. 11-26)

Therefore:
+ Repent
+ Indicative precedes imperative
+ Opportunistic

Leading a Bible study
Title: 'The Triumphant Indicative'
Text: Acts 3

(1) Introduce the issues
God verifies Peter's message as his gospel. The apostolic gospel preached at Pentecost, and repeated in Acts 3, is God's gospel and bears his eternal warranty.

(2) Study the passage

Acts 3:1-26

i)   Acts 2:43 says that the apostles did many miraculous signs. Why is the healing of the crippled beggar so outstanding (v. 16)?

ii)   What is ironic about the beggar's state and place?

iii)   What does Luke emphasise in verses 7-9 about the beggar?

iv)   What does this miracle show us about the continuing ministry of the ascended Christ (v. 16; Luke 5:17ff)?

v)   How does Peter expose the enormity of Israel's sin in crucifying Jesus (vv. 11-16)?

vi)   What must Israel do and what will follow (vv. 17-21)?

vii)   How is Jesus described in these verses? What is Israel's great advantage over the nations?

(3) Think it through

i)   How else do we explain this beggar's complete healing except that it happened (just as those most immediately involved maintained), all because of Jesus.

ii)   The resurrection of Jesus and all the other signs, like the healing of this beggar, accredit the apostolic gospel as God's truth.

(4) Live it out

i)   Since the gospel is accredited, how does that affect our confidence in God to do his saving work through it?

ii)   Like Paul in Romans 1:16, we can say we are not ashamed of the gospel. How do we show our lack of shame?

iii)   The gospel is God's truth, God's momentous news. How does this affect the way we think about it and what we do with it?

8

'HANDLING HOSTILITY'

'Who Pulls The Strings And Who Speaks The Truth?'
(ACTS 4:1-31; 5:17-42)

Listening to the text

'In this world, trouble…'. That's the promise of Jesus to the disciples gathered together on the night before his crucifixion (John 16:33). Just as crowds and preaching go together in Acts, so does the world and trouble!

The world will tolerate the church only when it is the type of church it finds tolerable. The church the world likes is the 'qualifying' church – the church that says 'perhaps' or 'maybe', the church that constantly asserts 'we are not being dogmatic'. It is the church that is strong on social involvement (as long as that doesn't extend to criticism of social policy), but weak on gospel proclamation. When the world says: 'We love your type of Church, your style of Christianity', then the alarm bells ought to be ringing.

The church in Acts never had that kind of trouble. At the outset it is characterised by dynamic growth (4:4), bold proclamation (4:8-12), and a vivid demonstration of supernatural power (4:16). Everybody living in Jerusalem had heard about the healing of the congenitally paralysed forty year-old, who now walks, jumps and praises God. That includes the Sanhedrin who confer together and decide to intervene!

Here in Acts 4, the Sanhedrin represents the world of hostility. It is the same body that dealt with the case of Jesus (Matt. 26:57ff). Here they deal with Peter and John. In chapter 7, they will deal with Stephen, then in chapter 23, with Paul. As the ruling Council of Judaism, the Sanhedrin, made up of Pharisees and Sadducees, had authority in all areas of Jewish life. Of particular significance was their role as guardians of religious orthodoxy.

The pattern evident here will recur again and again through Acts: where there is gospel advance, there will be some form of opposition. In terms of structure, there are five movements in the narrative:

+ the opponents (4:1-7);
+ Peter's address (4:8-12);
+ the opponents (4:13-22);
+ the church's response (4:23-30);
+ the summary (4:31).

(1) Movement 1: the opponents (4:1-7)

In verse 1, Luke introduces the ruling superstructure of the day: the priests, the captain of the temple guard and the Sadducees. The priests were responsible for all the activity in the temple, the temple guards for the maintenance of order in the temple and the Sadducees, as the ruling class in Israel, were particularly concerned to maintain healthy relationships with the Roman authorities. Their concerns were both theological and political. Theologically, the Sadducees didn't believe in an after-life, and were disturbed by the proclamation of the resurrection of the dead through Jesus (v. 2). Politically, because people were joining those proclaiming Christ in the temple daily, Rome might view the growing sect as a dangerous movement that could stir-up political unrest in the region and disturb the uneasy balance within Judaism that allowed it to co-exist with Imperial rule. In this potent mix, the ruling elite were not merely concerned, but greatly disturbed (v. 2).

Their tactic, in common with most political opposition, is to impose silence. And the quickest way to achieve this was imprisonment of the key protagonists (v. 3). This was the first of many occasions the apostles would find themselves in prison. But Luke reminds us that even as the opponents get a head of steam, God continues to do his work (v. 4).

The next day, Luke records, the august body of the Sanhedrin gather (v. 5). They have one question: 'By what power or what name did you do this?' We must not miss the irony of the situation: the leaders of God's people simply have no idea of what the God they profess to worship is doing.

(2) Movement 2: Peter's address (4:8-12)
Peter stands before the tribunal, but like Stephen in chapter 7, he does not act like the accused. Rather, he goes on to the front foot. The Sanhedrin becomes the accused, as Peter 'filled with the Holy Spirit' (v. 8), delivers a three point sermon:

+ Point 1: Jesus Christ of Nazareth is responsible for the healing (v. 10). This healed paralytic didn't heal himself.
+ Point 2: Jesus is alive and in the place of authority. They (i.e. the Sanhedrin and all the people of Israel)

crucified Jesus; but God raised him from the dead (v. 10). Peter quotes their own scriptures to them. Jesus is the chief cornerstone in God's building, the one central to the fulfilment of God's purposes. Yet he is the one they rejected (v. 11).

+ Point 3: Jesus is the unique Saviour (v. 12), the one who raised this man and gave him the ability to walk. He is the one who will lead God's people to the centre of all God's purposes, announce forgiveness of sin, and pour out the gift of the Holy Spirit.

+ Conclusion: There is only one way to God and Jesus is that way. To reject Jesus is to reject God.

Acts 4:12 is a timely reminder to us of the uniqueness of Christ. There is no other who can save: '...no one else... no other name'. Such a statement makes it clear that Christianity is not one way amongst many to God. If the Christian faith is true, then all the other faiths must be false because there is 'no other name'. The basis of such a claim is that he is the one who died, was raised and was exalted to God's right hand. Further proof for the truth of the claim is the crippled beggar standing healed before them. The ascended Christ is still active.

When John the Baptist doubted whether Jesus was the Christ, he asked the right question: 'Are you the one who was to come or should we expect someone else' (Matt. 11:2)? If Jesus is not the way, or not the sole way, who else has done what he did? Should we still be looking for another? The answer of the gospel is, 'no one else...no other name'.

Peter's address is brilliantly succinct and clear, yet he is a theological novice, a fisherman with no formal training, speaking to the political and religious elite of Israel. Luke makes it clear that the apostles' capacity for such bold proclamation is the power of the Holy Spirit (v 8). Peter and John have been in jail for the night. Now they respond to hostility with clear proclamation, in the power provided by the Spirit.

(3) Movement 3: the opponents (4:13-22)

Again Luke records the response of the audience. They are astonished that such insight comes from unschooled men, although they had met such insight before in Jesus' preaching, and note that these men had been with Jesus (v. 13). They are speechless (v. 14). What could they say? The man standing there healed was testimony to what Peter had said.

So, like all good religious bureaucracies, they form a committee (v. 15)! They engage in open discussion and then move, second and agree that the apostles be ordered to 'speak no longer to anyone in this name' (v. 17). That's the way opponents of disturbing truth seek to deal with it. They demand silence, so as to make the uncomfortable truth disappear, to change the reality and try to make everything go back to the way it was.

But they were caught on the horns of a real dilemma. If they punished Peter further, how would that look to the people? After all, the apostles had broken no law and had performed a great act of mercy that was obvious to all (v. 16).

Peter and John then put a radical question to the Sanhedrin (v. 19). Should we obey you and be silent, or obey God and speak about what we have seen and heard? This is a completely new proposition for the Sanhedrin. Until this moment, to obey God in Israel was to obey them; to hear the voice of God was to hear the Sanhedrin. But these men were saying that Jesus is the Lord and Christ, and that their allegiance, as God-honouring men, was to him, the one who had commissioned them (Acts 1:8). Whom should they obey?

To obey Jesus is to obey God! This testimony is repeated in 5:29. The Jewish leadership's own argument before Roman courts was exactly this; that their ultimate authority was no human court, but God alone. Peter and John now use the same argument against them!

The Sanhedrin make further threats and let them go (v. 21). It is significant that their response to the apostles and their gospel is neither reasoned debate and logical argument, nor an enquiring search for more detail. This is in direct contrast to the apostles, whose Spirit-empowered witness is seen in their determination to speak of what they have seen and heard. Who has the stronger case, the one who wishes to talk it out, or the one who wishes to impose silence?

(4) Movement 4: the church's response (4:22-30)

The church prays. They remind themselves that God is the sovereign Lord, the author of all (v. 24). Nothing happens apart from his control. This is the most comforting truth for the believer.

They remind themselves of the Spirit-inspired words of Scripture (vv. 25-26), which teach that there will be those who stand and plot against the Lord and his anointed (Ps. 2). In this case, those who stand and plot against Yahweh and his anointed are the Jewish hierarchy.

Prayer then, focusing on the sovereignty of God, sustained by Scripture, is the church's response to hostility.

Verse 27 provides the key to the application of Psalm 2 in this case. The plotters are Herod, Pilate, the Gentiles and the people of Israel. The human players are therefore put in their place. The Lord's anointed is Jesus, the Christ.

In prayer, the believers show how they understand the hostility in the light of the character of God and the evidence of Scripture (v. 28). However bad things may look, nothing happens for the people of God outside of God's superintendence. That was the case with Joseph being sold by his brothers (Gen. 50:20), Jesus being crucified (Acts 2:23) and now these threats by a hostile Sanhedrin. And lest we think that this truth only applied then, to them, we must remember that Paul assures us of its general application to those who love him and are called according to his purpose (Rom. 8:28).

The church then asks for boldness to speak and for God to continue to show the accreditation of the message (vv. 29-30). It is important to note that the recognition of God's sovereignty is not understood by the church to be an excuse for inactivity. The foundation of all activity – indeed, the reason why we pray – is that God is sovereign, so he is in control, and through prayer he will work and bless his people.

(5) Movement 5: the summary (4:31)

Like chapter 12, this is a chapter of contrasts. It begins with the Jewish hierarchy seeking to impose a blanket of silence, but ends with the Lord's laughter from heaven scoffing at them, the bold testimony of the Spirit-filled church, and the shaking of the place where they met (v. 31). What a sharp contrast between the sovereign Lord empowering bold proclamation by his people and the dead religious superstructure seeking to silence news of the Lord's saving work! The evidence for the Lord Jesus' saving work from heaven is publicly displayed in the healed man, for all Jerusalem to see, and publicly proclaimed by the apostles for all Jerusalem to hear. But the Sanhedrin, the supposed spiritual leaders of Israel, can do neither. They are blind and deaf.

From text to teaching
(1) Get the message clear
Big idea (theme)
The church must face hostility with bold, Spirit-inspired proclamation, strengthened by the conviction that God will see his purposes triumph.

Big question(s) (aim)
Hostility caused by the proclamation of Christ is the key issue in Acts 4. Preaching or teaching on this passage should answer the following questions:
+ How should we face hostility to proclaiming Christ?
+ Where does bold proclamation come from?
+ What is God's response to those who rail against him?

(2) Engage the Hearer
Point of contact
One contact point could be to raise the question: 'Have you ever been to court? How did it feel?' After reflecting on some people's court experiences, make the following general point: the more august the body, the greater the fear. Yet in this passage in Acts, we see the very opposite occurring. Previously, Peter denied Christ before a girl at the High

Priest's door (John 18:17), before the servants and officials of the High Priest's house (John 18:25) and before one of the High Priest's servants (John 18:26-27). Yet here Peter proclaims Christ not just before the High Priest himself, but before all the rulers of Israel. And he does so with boldness and courage. Why? What has changed?

Another contact point could be to give examples of visible evidence which show the presence of something invisible. For example, the effects of wind (both benign and destructive) showing the existence of air; a wedding ring (and corresponding visible acts of service) showing the existence of a marriage; orderly movements of traffic (most of the time) showing the existence of an agreed body of law governing road usage. From these examples the question can be raised, 'What will be the visible evidence of the Spirit's invisible presence with his people?' This section of Acts shows that one of the crucial visible evidences is courage and boldness in proclaiming Christ, even in the context of severe opposition and hostility. Can we expect such visible evidence to be apparent in the lives of believers today?

Dominant picture(s)
Unschooled, ordinary men address the mighty ruling body of Israel with boldness and insight. Expounding and explaining this powerful image in Acts 4 can be used by God to inspire similar boldness and courage in his people today.

(3) *Work on application*
Necessary application(s)
We must face up to hostility to the gospel with bold proclamation of Christ, empowered by the Holy Spirit, trusting in the sovereign oversight of God.

Refute impossible application(s)

We must reject the position advocated all too frequently by Christians publicly and privately in response to pressure not to proclaim Christ; which is that 'silence, letting my life do the talking, serves God best before a hostile world.' The Holy Spirit does not empower his people to silence.

Possible application(s)

Is prayer my first response to hostility? J.B. Phillips in his 'Translator's Preface' to *The Young Church in Action*, says of the church in Acts that '…they were open on the Godward side in a way that is almost unknown today'. He continues, 'they did not "say their prayers", they really prayed'. Do I really pray? Do I expect to experience bold speech as the evidence of his filling in response to prayer?

Proclaiming the message
A preaching outline

Title: 'Handling Hostility'

Texts: **Acts 4:1-31; 5:17-42**

Introduction: Fear in the face of hostile authorities

The difference the Spirit makes

… to the church in Luke's day:

- The opponents (vv. 1-7)
- Peter's address (vv 8-12)
- The opponents (vv. 13-22)
- The church's response (vv. 23-30)
- The summary (vv. 31)

... to the church in our day:
- ◆ Spirit-empowered proclamation
- ◆ Prayerful dependence
- ◆ Refusal to be silent

Conclusion: How will you and your church face hostility to proclaiming Christ?

Leading a Bible study
Title: **'Handling Hostility'**
Texts: **Acts 4:1-31; 5:17-42**

(1) Introduce the issues
Discuss a situation where you had to face hostility. How did it affect you? What temptations did you face?

(2) Study the passage
Acts 4:1-31

i)   Who were the opponents, why were they so upset and what did they do about it (vv. 1-3)?

ii) Why does Luke go to the trouble of identifying those involved (see Luke 23:10)?

iii) Why is the question in verse 7 so ironic?

iv) What stands out for you from Peter's response (vv. 8-14)? What does Luke emphasise?

v)   What do we learn about hostility to God's cause from verses 3, 17, 18, 21?

vi) What does the believers' prayer in verses 24-30 teach us about:
- ◆ how to pray in such a situation;
- ◆ the place of God's sovereignty and the use of Scripture in prayer;
- ◆ what to ask for when threatened with such hostility?

vii) Hostility to the gospel is real. How does verse 31 encourage us as we face hostility?

viii) What do you think is significant about Peter's use of scripture in verse 11 and the church's use of it in verses 25-26?

(3) *Think it through*
Taking 'proclamation' in its widest sense (from private conversations one-to-one through to public preaching before crowds), discuss the following questions with reference to:
   + you personally
   + your church corporately.

i) Which people with authority put (or would put) pressure on you not to proclaim Christ as the exclusive Saviour and Lord of all?

ii) What reasons are (or would be) cited for actively discouraging such proclamation?

(4) *Live it out*
i) To what extent do you actually face hostility for proclaiming Christ? What might this show?

ii) How can you respond to your situation in ways that reflect the early church's commendable example in Acts 4?

iii) What might be the outcome if you were to follow more fully the early church's example?

9

'TELLING LIES TO GOD'

(ACTS 4:32-5:11)

Listening to the text

Here is an example of Luke's 'warts and all' portrait of the early Christian church. Luke holds up a realistic mirror to the church, and shows God's commitment to root out sin in the church's earliest days. The first recorded sin in the new covenant community concerns a wealth issue. Wherever wealth is involved, sin is not far away. In this case, there was tension over the use of earthly possessions. The next incident is also about possessions. The grumbling of the widows in chapter 6 requires the church to address the issue of unequal distribution of welfare.

(1) Economic implications of the gospel (4:32-35)

We are first introduced to the economic implications of the gospel in the prototype church in chapter 2. Something like a Spirit-led voluntary socialism was operative. 'Selling their possessions and goods, they gave to anyone as he had need' (Acts 2:45). Again, here in chapter 4, we are reminded that no one claimed private ownership, but that everything was shared (v. 32). Consequently, 'there were no needy persons among them' (v. 34). Private ownership was recognized, but apparently no one pressed their rights. Not only was the eradication of needy persons in their midst a result of generous giving, it also involved the sale of capital items – houses and land – and the money from such sales was laid at the apostles' feet. So they weren't just sharing from their income but were sacrificing capital. Their sharing was selfless (v. 32), sacrificial (vv. 34-35) and voluntary (vv. 32, 34-37). There was no law imposing these standards – this sharing arose from a desire to live this way.

For the Greeks, such common ownership was an 'ideal' which, it was thought, would lead to oneness of spirit. Acts shows it is the other way around: oneness of spirit leads to common ownership. Luke emphasises this in 4:31: 'And they were all filled with the Holy Spirit…' The Spirit helped them to value people over possessions. This is an outstanding picture from another world.

(2) Barnabas (4:36-37; 11:19-24, 25-26; 13:2, 42, 46; 14:23; 15:2, 12; 15:37-39)

Luke then introduces Joseph, the Levite from Cyprus. He has been nicknamed Barnabas by the apostles, which means 'the encourager'. Every mention of him in Acts is one of encouragement: his appointment by the church in Jerusalem is intended to encourage the Gentile church in Antioch (11:19-24), he searches for Saul in Tarsus and asks him to join him in discipling the new believers (11:25-26), he is set apart with Saul for the first missionary journey (13:2) where he is the initial leader of the pair - Paul's giftedness leads Luke to refer to 'Paul and Barnabas' thereafter (13:42,

46; 14:23). It's been said: 'It takes more grace than I can tell you to play the second fiddle well'. Barnabas again takes the lead before the Jerusalem council (15:2, 12). It is Barnabas who perseveres with John Mark when Paul's patience has run out (15:37-39). He is one of those who sells property, a field, and lays the entire amount at the apostles' feet for distribution (4:37).

(3) Ananias and Sapphira (5:1-11)

The husband and wife Ananias and Sapphira also sold property and, acting in concert, laid part of the proceeds at the apostles' feet while keeping back some for themselves (5:2). As Peter says, they were quite free to keep the lot, or put any portion of the sale at the church's disposal (v. 4). But what they did was lay the portion down as if it were the whole amount. They wanted to gain the same reputation for generosity as Barnabas and the others had, while keeping some of the cash for themselves. We are not told how Peter found out about this, but there is clear parallel to God's knowledge of the first sin in the old covenant community when they entered the Promised Land. This incident also involved wealth. Achan kept back devoted plunder for himself (Josh. 7), but God knew. His judgment on Achan and his family was instant and complete, as was his judgment on Ananias and Sapphira in the new covenant community. God never hates sin so much as when he finds it amongst his own people.

Peter makes it clear that this act of hypocrisy was inspired by Satan (5:3); constituted a lie to the Holy Spirit (v. 3) and to God (v. 4); and was considered by the Spirit of the Lord to be testing him (v. 9). Ananias and Sapphira believed the lie that they could buy themselves a reputation;

the work they presented was a counterfeit of the work of the Holy Spirit. Their actions sprang from the pride of their hearts. They were inspired by the Devil, the father of lies, the father of the fake (John 8:44). The irony is that they do make a reputation – down through the centuries Ananias and Sapphira have become names synonymous with hypocrisy.

God's judgment is swift. First Ananias died and the young men carried him out for burial (vv. 5-6). Three hours later, when Sapphira made it clear she was one with her husband in the lie, she died and the same young men carried her out (v. 9). Great fear seized the church (vv. 5, 11), and no doubt a good deal of self-examination occurred to rid themselves of every vestige of fakery and hypocrisy from their lives. God removes this threat to the church so the work can go on. The church is to be the environment where the lie cannot live. This is to be the authentic, Spirit-filled community, not the Satanic fake.

From text to teaching
(1) Get the message clear
Big idea (theme)
The unity and fellowship of believers is a result of the Holy Spirit's work, but when it is mimicked for personal glory, it is a lie to God.

Big question(s) (aim)
Preaching or teaching on this passage should answer the following questions:

+ When is our unity and fellowship a lie to God?
+ What does it mean to lie to God?
+ How can we identify a counterfeit?

(2) Engage the hearer
Point of contact

We have all had experience of someone playing a part, when a person pretends to be something they are not. For example, there are numerous stories of people who have set up practice as a doctor even though they have no medical qualifications. There is the amusing story of the young engineer, Matthew Richardson, who shared the same name as a Professor of Economics in the United States. The engineer Richardson was mistakenly invited to give a series of lectures on Economics in China. He accepted the invitation, read up on basic economics and went and gave the lectures! Any story of an 'imposter', of someone putting on a mask, can be used as a point of contact for teaching from this section of Acts.

Dominant picture(s)

The narrative gives us a terrible picture of the awesome judgment of the holy God – in this case upon fakers. You can ask your hearers to think about the event from the perspective of the young men burying Ananias and then Sapphira within three hours of one another. It is a fearful picture. If you had been there you would talk about it for a long time.

(3) Work on application
Necessary application(s)

We must repent of every vestige of hypocrisy and live in Spirit-inspired open integrity before God and before one another. James 4:7: 'Submit yourselves, then, to God. Resist the devil, and he will flee from you'. Literally, put yourself under God and put yourself over the Devil, who is the source and inspirer of all fakery.

Refute impossible application(s)
An impossible application would be to continue excusing sin in the church on the basis that it contains a mixture of people, including 'Barnabases', 'Ananiases' and 'Sapphiras'. Another would be that I can rest on God's acceptance of me 'just the way I am', as a mixture of godliness and sinfulness, so that I become complacent about sin in my life. Rather, God shows his sensitivity to our sin by calling us to continually repent as we examine ourselves in the light of his Word.

Possible application(s)
Remember that wealth can be a wonderful servant of the purposes of God – see the example of Barnabas and others (Acts 4:32-36). But wealth can also be a monstrous master – it contorts, perverts and exposes our fakery (Acts 5:1-11).

We live in prosperous times, but the Spirit will help us to value people over possessions. Such valuation will show itself in practical help given to the needy and by an open door of hospitality into our comfortable homes.

Paul calls idolatry – the worship of the created, not the Creator – 'the lie' (Rom. 1:25). There is no greater lie than idolatry, and there is no more persistent and insidious idol than wealth. The material is a powerful idol. It can be seen and touched, it attracts power and status, it brings security and comfort. This idol has captured the Western church. It needs to be smashed. Giving destroys the idol of wealth. If God's Spirit has convicted you about wealth management, then smash the idol by prayerful, thoughtful, strategic self-sacrificial generosity.

But also remember that there can be a trap in giving. We may give for wrong reasons such as public approval, reputation and status! Similarly, we need to remember that there is a trap in hoarding. Jesus said that what we hoard captures our heart and masters us (Matt. 6:19-24). Jesus repeats: 'no-one can ... you cannot ...' (Matt. 6:24). So rule your wealth in the name of Jesus by the power of his Holy Spirit, and don't let it rule you.

Proclaiming the message
A preaching outline
Title: 'Telling Lies To God'
Text: Acts 4:32-5:11

(1) The gospel's economy
- selfless (4:32)
- voluntary (4:34-35)
- sacrificial (4:34-35)

   Barnabas the model, among others (4:36-37)
   Its inspiration (4:31)

(2) The Satanic fake
   Ananias and Sapphira in concert (5:1-2, 8)
   Its inspiration (5:3)
   Its constitution
- the lie (5:3-4)
- testing the Spirit (5:9)
   God's swift judgment (5:5, 9) (like Achan, Josh. 7)

(3) Beware of the lie – the idolatry of wealth

Leading a Bible study
Title: 'Telling Lies To God'
Text: Acts 4:32-5:11

(1) Introduce the issues
Luke introduces us to the economic implications of the gospel. Something like a Spirit-inspired voluntary socialism was operative in the early church. However, wherever wealth is involved, sin is not far away. Ananias and Sapphira show that problems arise when we hoard wealth. Hypocrisy can also take root in the way we give away wealth.

(2) Study the passage
Acts 4:32-5:11

i)   Kruschev said: 'Communism's failure is its failure to produce the selfless man'. Where does the selflessness of 4:32-37 come from?

ii)   What can we learn about Barnabas here and in 11:25-27; 13:2; 13:42; 15:37-41?

iii)   What evidence can you find that Ananias and Sapphira acted together?

iv)   Who motivated them? (v. 3) Why is this typical of his work? (see John 8:44).

v)   What Ananias and Sapphira did is called a lie (v. 4) and a test (v. 9). Why?

vi)   Why was God's judgment so instantaneous in this case?

vii)   How do you think, the 'great fear' of the church (v. 11) may have shown itself in their daily lives?

(3) Think it through
Hypocrisy, or playing a part, is always unacceptable to God. How are we apt to be hypocrites today (see Matt. 6:1-18)?

(4) Live it out

i)   The Western church is weighed down with the forces of materialism, consumerism and wealth accumulation. How can we smash the idol of wealth?

ii) Think of ways in which wealth can be a wonderful servant of the gospel, but a dangerous master in our lives.

10
'So The Word Of God Spread'

(Acts 6:1-7)

Listening to the text

Luke uses different methods to indicate what is important and what he thinks of the events he recounts in his narrative. One method is his use of repetition. In particular, Luke provides a comment on the health of the ministry of the Word of God three times in Acts. We will take them in reverse order.

(1) The Word spreads – occurrence three

The third repetition comes in Acts 19:20: 'In this way the word of the Lord spread widely and grew in power'. This statement comes at the conclusion of Paul's pioneer church planting work, culminating in the church plant at Ephesus. As Paul lays down his missionary mantle, Luke names no less than ten of Paul's co-workers in the next thirty verses to show that though Paul's pioneering work is finished, the work of the gospel is not finished (you can read their names in 19:22, 29; 20:4). The ministry of the Word is bigger than any human personality.

In chapter 19 the Sons of Sceva try to use the name of Jesus to drive out evil spirits. They refer to 'Jesus' (v. 13), and the evil spirit refers to 'Jesus' (v. 15), but when Luke refers to Jesus, it is as the 'Lord Jesus' (vv. 13, 17). The sons' fakery is exposed when the evil spirit overpowers them – the spirit is not fooled, beats them and exposes them to public ridicule. This has such an impact that even believers who had been dabbling in sorcery immediately burn their magic scrolls. Superstitious fakery will not flourish, but God's Word will flourish. As the scrolls burn, the Word spreads and grows.

(2) *The Word spreads – occurrence two*

The second reference to the health of the ministry of the Word is in Acts 12:24: 'But the word of God continued to increase and spread'. Here the Word's health is contrasted with the wormy diseased demise of the political opportunist, Herod. Herod had taken his stand against the church, had James martyred and Peter arrested. But God takes his stand against Herod – the angel who struck Peter awake in prison (v. 7) now strikes Herod down so that 'he was eaten with worms and died' (v. 23). Seemingly indomitable political power will not flourish, but the Word of God will increase and spread.

(3) *The Word spreads – first occurrence*

This brings us back to the first reference to the health of the ministry of the Word in Acts 6:7: 'So the word of God spread'. Here the contrast is not with spiritual fakery or political power, but with the health of the church as it deals with an internal welfare issue. The Greek-speaking Jews from regions outside Jerusalem complain (the Greek word is onomatopoeic, *gongusmos*) against the Hebraic Jews from Jerusalem because their widows were being overlooked in the daily distribution of welfare. This oversight was probably accidental rather than deliberate, yet it had the potential to disrupt the unity of the church. So the leadership of the apostles was prompt, they 'gathered all the disciples' (v. 2).

Church disunity always has the potential to slow down the flow of the gospel, as a fractured church is rarely missionary focused and evangelistic in orientation. Disunity saps our emotional resources – we are so busily engaged within the fellowship that we have no strength left to reach out.

The apostles are open and transparent (v. 2), recognising that the ministry of the Word of God must not be neglected because of the need to minister to the widows. The apostles' ministry involves prayer and the ministry of the Word (v. 4).

This continues to be the primary responsibility of the church leader today. Many worthy ministry pressures will crowd out these priorities. We must constantly remember that 'the main thing is that the main thing remains the main thing.' To wait on tables is good, but it is not, for the apostles, the main thing. It is also important to recognise that in assessing the various demands in ministry it is not a case of the good and the bad. It is more a case of the best and the good, and prioritising between the best and the good takes real biblical nerve. Waiting on tables is good, but for the apostles it has the potential to take them away from the Word and prayer, which for them was their best.

The widespread nature of Christian ministry provides a way of meeting the pressing need of the widows and preserving the apostles for their primary ministry: 'Brothers,

choose seven men…' (v. 3). Note that even for this welfare
task, fullness of the Spirit and wisdom are necessary (v. 3).
An election takes place (vv. 5-6), and where we might have
expected a ratio of five Hebrew to two Greek deacons, or
vice versa, in fact seven men with Greek names and no
Hebrew-speaking believers are selected! By this means the
church shows its sensitive awareness of the threat presented
to its unity by this issue. Now there will be no vestige of
discrimination against the Greek-speaking widows.

The result of this election was that grumbling did not
spread, but the Word of God did (v. 7). Not only did it spread
widely, but deeply – even the Sanhedrin was penetrated so
that a 'large number of priests became obedient to the faith'.

(4) *Summary*

God prospers his Word through the single-minded
leadership of the apostles. Superstitious fakery did not
spread, the Word of God did. Political power did not
increase, the Word of God did. Complaining dissension did
not grow, the Word of God did. By use of contrast Luke
shows the health and strength of God's Word and therefore
God's cause.

From text to teaching

(1) *Get the message clear*

Big idea *(theme)*

God will see his Word triumph in the face of grumbling
dissension, political opportunism and superstitious fakery.

Big question(s) *(aim)*

Preaching or teaching on this passage should answer the
following question: how does God prosper his Word and

fulfil his purpose? Answer: through the zealous (single-minded) leadership of the apostles.

(2) *Engage the hearer*
Point of contact
Some lessons are so vivid that you remember the precise circumstances you were in when you learned them. I remember the grazier who told me, 'As you find the gate, so leave it after you drive through. If it's open when you find it, leave it that way; if it's closed, leave it that way too.' I remember the mechanic who told me, 'Every tool has a place, use it and return it to that place. Time is money.' When I was a new pastor in my first parish, facing the pressing needs of a large congregation and not knowing where to start, I read the words of the American church historian Martyn Marty: 'The main thing is that the main thing remains the main thing'.

Dominant picture
Gongusmos-ing dissension (the word is powerfully onomatopoetic!) is contrasted with clear, single-minded, transparent leadership. When dissension stops, the Word spreads widely and penetrates deeply.

(3) *Work on application*
Necessary application(s)
It is ironic that in a book called 'Acts', the power of the 'Word' is so emphasised. Jesus single-mindedly set his face for Jerusalem; Christian leaders are to be similarly determined and single-minded, not giving in to pressure to engage in ministry other than that of Word and prayer. All Israel's failures resulted from a failure of leadership. Her leaders

lost focus on Yahweh and that infected their every decision. Today's leaders must zealously lead with God's priorities. God will honour such leadership.

Refute impossible application(s)

The example of the apostles in this passage refutes the view that God's Word will flourish without any help or leadership from us. It also flies in the face of all calls for ministry to adapt to the current perceived needs of the twenty-first century church in a bid to be more relevant. This may be pressure to allow the counselling couch to displace the pulpit, or for preaching to adapt to the march of secular consumerism by offering power, prestige and prosperity. Listen to what Bishop Ryle said about single-mindedness:

> 'A zealous man in religion is pre-eminently *a man of one thing*. It is not enough to say that he is earnest, hearty, uncompromising, thorough-going, whole-hearted, fervent in spirit. He only sees one thing, he only cares for one thing, he lives for one thing, he is swallowed up in one thing; and that one thing is to please God. Whether he lives, or whether he dies, – whether he has health, or whether he has sickness, – whether he is rich, or whether he is poor, – whether he pleases man, or whether he gives offence, – whether he is thought wise, or whether he is thought foolish, – whether he gets blame, or whether he gets praise, – whether he gets honour, or whether he gets shame, – for all this the zealous man cares nothing at all. He burns for one thing; and that one thing is to please God,

and to advance God's glory. If he is consumed in the very burning, he cares not for it, he is content. He feels that, like a lamp, he is made to burn; and if consumed in burning, he has but done the work for which God appointed him. Such a one will always find a sphere for his zeal. If he cannot preach, and work, and give money, he will cry, and sigh, and pray. Yes: if he is only a pauper, on a perpetual bed of sickness, he will make the wheels of sin around him drive heavily, by continually interceding against it. If he cannot fight in the valley with a Joshua, he will do the work of Moses, Aaron, and Hur, on the hill. (Exod. 17:9-13.) If he is cut off from working himself, he will give the Lord no rest till help is raised up from another quarter, and the work is done. This is what I mean when I speak of 'zeal' in religion' (from J. C. Ryle's "Sermon on Zeal" in *Practical Religion*). **May God give us the zeal to see that the main thing remains the main thing.**

Possible application(s)

A great pressure on pastoral leadership is to be responsive to the unrealistic expectations of our people and not do the very thing God has set us apart to do. One major cause of clergy drop-out is the pressure felt by pastors to conform to people's unrealistic expectations of what they should do.

One pastor promised at his induction never to stand before his people with a half-baked sermon. He established the 'main thing'; his challenge was then to maintain it as the main thing.

Proclaiming the message
A preaching outline
Title: 'So The Word Of God Spread'
Texts: Acts 19:20; 12:24; 6:1-7

(1) The Word grew – superstitious fakery did not
     (Acts 19:20)
(2) The Word grew – naked political ambition did not
     (Acts 12:24)
(3) Acts 6:1-7
     + two groups (v. 1)
     + leadership (v. 2)
     + prompt
     + open
     + recognised priority (vv. 2, 4)
     + widespread nature of ministry (v. 3)
     + the election (vv. 5-6)
     + the result (v. 7)
(4) The Word grew – grumbling did not
(5) The main thing is that the main thing remains the
     main thing.

Leading a Bible study
Title: 'So The Word Of God Spread'
Texts: Acts 19:20; 12:24; 6:1-7

(1) Introduce the issues
In Acts, Luke stresses the health of the Word in contrast
to the failure of political manoeuvring and superstitious
fakery outside the church, and internal grumbling within.
No matter what the world throws at us, God will always see
his purposes triumph.

(2) Study the passages

Acts 19:13-20; 12:21-24; 6:1-7

i)   What is being contrasted with the health of the Word in the Acts 19 passage?

ii) What is being contrasted with the health of the Word in the Acts 12 passage?

iii) What are the qualities of apostolic leadership on display in Acts 6?

iv) Did the apostles view table ministry as inferior (v. 2)?

v)   What constitutes a ministry of the Word and prayer?

vi) What is significant about the result of the election (vv. 5-6)?

vii) Why is it significant that so many priests became obedient to the faith (v. 7)?

viii) Acts 6:7; 12:24; 19:20 are all similar. What do they tell us about God's cause?

(3) Think it through

On two of these three occasions God intervenes directly and brings about the healthy growth of his Word (ch. 12, 19). In chapter 6, God uses the single-minded leadership of his apostles to bring about the spread of the Word. What does this teach us about the place of godly leadership in God's purposes?

(4) Live it out

i)   To what extent could our leadership be described as single-minded?

ii) What is to be my single-minded concern?

iii) What is to be our church's single-minded concern?

iv) What are the enemies of single-mindedness?

v)   By contrast, how do narrow-mindedness, double-
     mindedness and small-mindedness show themselves
     in the life of our church and in our personal lives?

SERIES TWO:

The Word Spreads!

Acts 6:8-13:3

11

'THE CHURCH'S FIRST MARTYR'

(ACTS 6:8-8:1)

Listening to the text

The martyrdom of Stephen is a major turning point in the narrative of Acts. It introduces us to Saul and is in itself the means God uses to get the gospel out of Judea and into Samaria. The widespread scattering of disciples to Samaria (Acts 8:1) leads also to the establishment of the Gentile church in Antioch (Acts 11:19-20).

(1) Setting and background

Stephen's name means 'crown'. Luke gives us a very full account of the circumstances surrounding his death. Stephen is one of the deacons elected in Acts 6:5. Luke describes him as full of the Spirit and wisdom (6:3), full of faith and the Holy Spirit (6:5), a man full of God's grace and power (6:8). To 'be full of' means to be 'under the control of'. God gave him the ability to perform wonders and signs (v. 8) and to speak with insight (v. 10). In Luke's portrait there are striking similarities between Stephen and Moses, such as their power and wisdom in dealing with authorities.

(2) *Charges against Stephen*

Opposition comes from the synagogue. Stephen must have had a teaching, preaching ministry for the synagogue to take exception to his activity. Stephen's opponents soon abandon argument when they realise they can't 'out-debate' Stephen, and resort to more underhand methods. They stir up opposition, secretly persuading men to be false witnesses against him (vv. 11-13).

Stephen teaches differently from the synagogue elders regarding Moses and the temple. But who is the preserver of the correct understanding of the law and temple? Is it the Sanhedrin/synagogue or is it Stephen? They lay a two-fold charge against Stephen before the Sanhedrin:

+ He speaks against Moses by speaking against his law (vv. 11, 13). He said that Jesus will change the customs of Moses (v. 14).
+ He speaks against God, by speaking against the temple (vv. 11, 13). He said that Jesus will destroy the temple (v. 14).

The people of Jerusalem would have been easily stirred by such charges, since their livelihood depended on the temple and the law (v. 12). The same charge was made against Jesus before the same Council. Mark 14:58: 'We heard him say, "I will destroy this man-made temple and in three days will build another, not made by man."' What Jesus actually said, however, was: 'Destroy this temple, and I will raise it again in three days' (John 2:19). No doubt Stephen would have referred to Jesus' words and explained how he was referring to the death and resurrection of his own body.

Verse 15 tells us that Stephen's face, like Moses at Sinai, shone like an angel (Exod. 34:29). Both Moses' ministry of law and Stephen's interpretation of it had the approval of God. Luke makes it clear with this reference and his description of Stephen that God's favour rests on Stephen as it rested on Moses.

(3) Stephen's defence speech

There follows in 7:1-53 the longest defence of Christianity in the New Testament. Yet, Stephen is in no way on the defensive – Israel and her leaders are at the bar of the tribunal and he lets their own history accuse them. The speech has three parts:

+ Verses 2-16, the period of the Patriarchs - Abraham, Isaac, Jacob and Joseph. It concludes with the deaths of Jacob and Joseph and with the people of Israel in Egypt.
+ Verses 17-43, the period covering Moses, the law, the Exodus and the wilderness wandering.
+ Verses 44-50 cover the place of the tabernacle and temple.

Remember that Stephen has been charged with blasphemy against Moses and God. Of course, Stephen relates to the Sanhedrin what they already know, but by selecting and organising his material he is making a strong point. He begins respectfully, verse 2, addressing them as brothers and fathers and stressing their common ancestor, Abraham. He makes the following points.

(i) Blasphemy against Moses

God's deliverers are consistently rejected by Israel: 'Because the patriarchs were jealous of Joseph they sold him as a slave into Egypt' (v. 9). Yet God was with Joseph, rescued him, and gave him wisdom and success. Even so he was sold as a slave, but when eventually he revealed himself to his family (v. 13), he was recognised as deliverer.

Moses was a beautiful child (v. 20); a bringer of peace and reconciliation. And yet, he too was rejected by his own (vv. 25-26). It was when they saw him a second time (v. 35) that he was recognised as deliverer. Yet, though he gave Israel the law and the covenant, God's living words (v. 38), they brushed him aside and rejected him in favour of an idol of a lifeless calf (v. 41).

True to form, the Sanhedrin has now rejected God's Righteous One (v. 52), just as the previous leadership of Israel rejected the prophets. Ironically, the One they have rejected was spoken of by Moses as the Prophet (v. 37 cf. Deut. 18:15). Clearly they can expect to see him a second time, when they will all too belatedly recognise him as deliverer.

(ii) Blasphemy against God and the temple

Israel has made an idol of the temple. Isaiah specifically taught that God cannot be localised in a building (vv. 48-50, cf. Isaiah 66:1-2). Yahweh is the God who is on the move; in Mesopotamia speaking to Abraham (v. 2), in Egypt with Joseph (v. 9), in the desert appearing to Moses (v. 30). God cannot be contained in one place.

Israel made the calf (v. 41) and then built the temple (v. 47). Despite Scripture's protestations, tabernacle and temple have become human attempts to contain God. The true God, Stephen asserts, is not static and localised, but is with his people. He makes them wise, is merciful and gives them success. He is dynamic and gives them living words. Israel contains and localises God, making idols of his temple and tabernacle. If then God is everywhere, empowering and merciful, who are the blasphemers of Moses and God?

(iii) Conclusion

In reality, the Sanhedrin are not Stephen's brothers (v. 2). Stephen uses Gentile descriptions for them; stiff-necked and uncircumcised (v. 51). There is no excuse for them: this brushing aside of Joseph, Moses, the prophets and the Lord Jesus was done in the face of their great privileges: '...you who have received the law that was put into effect through angels but have not obeyed it' (v. 53). The killing of the Righteous One was their greatest mistake (v. 52).

The biggest challenge to Moses' laws was, of course, Jesus. He was the Sabbath breaker, who declared all foods clean, who touched lepers and openly associated with sinners. The biggest challenge to the temple was also Jesus; he cleansed the temple and taught that he was the true temple, the meeting-place between men and God.

In this court the judge is the guilty criminal and is out of control with rage (v. 54). He takes the law into his own hands and illegally imposes capital punishment (v. 58).

Again heaven opens (v. 55 cf. 2:2) and Stephen sees Jesus, the Son of Man, standing at the right hand of God, to receive his first martyr. In his dying, Stephen is very similar to his Lord. He commits his spirit to the Lord Jesus (see Luke 23:46), prays for forgiveness for his killers (see Luke 23:34), and then falls asleep (v. 60). In stoning

Stephen, Israel maintains its consistent pattern in rejecting all Yahweh's messengers.

Luke finishes the account by telling us that Saul was there, that he had seen Stephen's face, and heard Stephen's words (8:1). Ironically, Saul was to become the most articulate advocate of Stephen's conservative respect for the traditions and his radical understanding of them. But for now, Saul gives approval to Stephen's death.

From text to teaching
(1) Get the message clear
Big idea (theme)
Both God and Israel are thoroughly consistent. God is dynamic and merciful - the pilgrim God. Israel has always sought to localise him and has rejected his messengers, culminating in their rejection of his Righteous One.

Big question(s) (aim)
Preaching or teaching on this passage should answer the following questions:

+ Where can I find God?
+ Who speaks truly for God?
+ Which constituency represents me, the Sanhedrin or Stephen?
+ Who is true to Moses and to God?

(2) Engage the hearer
Point of contact
We hate to be brushed aside. We dislike being brushed aside by total strangers. It is worse when friends and especially family members brush us aside. Today we will be with Stephen as he goes to court, accused by the leaders of his own nation.

However, it seems that no one has told him that he is the accused, because he acts as if he were the prosecuting attorney. To brush others aside is bad enough, but Stephen charges Israel with brushing aside all of God's messengers and finally brushing aside God himself, the Righteous One.

Dominant picture(s)

The scene is of a court room, but with switched roles. Stephen, charged before the national tribunal, does not act like the accused. Rather, he switches roles and becomes the prosecuting attorney with his accusers in the box.

(3) Work on application
Necessary application(s)

God's purposes, though seemingly suffering the setback of initial rejection, will ultimately triumph. He is the sovereign God who will sustain us as we persevere in ministry. His sovereign care, seeing his purpose triumph, is our greatest comfort.

Refute impossible application(s)

The following impossible applications might helpfully be stated and refuted:

+ that God can be localised in a building;
+ that God has a 'hands off' approach to the administration of his affairs;
+ that God's Spirit-filled servants can be assured of safety, security and prosperity.

Possible application(s)

Stephen, with his radical understanding of God and his ways, provides the Christian with a model for engaging the hostile world around us, boldly and filled with the Spirit.

We are to engage even if that world is the world of the religious 'brothers and fathers' with whom we share much in common (cf. v. 2).

Good, wise, powerful, godly servants of the poor, like Stephen, can be slandered, accused, abused, despised and killed by the guardians of God's traditions. We should not be surprised (John 15:20).

When we are brushed aside in the cause of the gospel, we are not to despair, for God's cause will triumph. Even an arch persecutor can become an apostle of that which he had previously hated. As Martin Luther could sing:

> 'And though they take our life,
> goods, honour, children, wife;
> Yet is their profit small,
> these things shall vanish all;
> The city of God remaineth.'

Beware of duplicating the biggest mistake of history and brushing off Jesus. For Christ's sake, all unworthy ambitions, dreams and goals should be brushed aside.

Proclaiming the message
A preaching outline

Title: **'The Church's First Martyr'**

Text: **Acts 6:8-8:1**

(1) **Two views of Moses** (Acts 6:8-7:2)
  - ✦ Stephen and his accusers (6:8-15)
    - He speaks against the law
    - He speaks against the temple
  - ✦ Stephen on the front foot (7:1-2)

(2) **The evidence of the Patriarchs** (7:2-16)
- ✦ God with Abraham – the promise of the law (vv. 2-8)
- ✦ God with Joseph – Israel in Egypt (vv. 9-16)

(3) **The evidence of the Exodus** (7:17-43)
- ✦ God with Moses   - preparation (vv. 17-29)
                                 - revelation (vv. 30-34)
                                 - rejection (vv. 35-43)

(4) **Tabernacle and Temple** (7:44-50)
- ✦ blasphemy against Moses – the law (vv. 44-46)
- ✦ blasphemy against God – the temple (vv. 47-50)

The Conclusion:
(5) **The pattern repeats** (7:51-8:1)
- ✦ For Jesus (7:51-53)
- ✦ For Stephen (7:54-8:1)

Leading a Bible study
Title: 'The Church's First Martyr'
Text: **Acts 6:8-8:1**

(1) Introduce the issues
Israel accused Stephen of blasphemy of God and of Moses, yet Israel has consistently brushed aside God's messengers, including Moses. By rejecting the Righteous One, the Lord Jesus, they have effectively rejected God himself. The issue is, who speaks for Moses - Stephen or the Sanhedrin?

The text also shows that Stephen's integrity does not exempt him from opposition, suffering and death at the hands of the Sanhedrin. What are our expectations for how God's servants will be treated?

(2) Study the passage
Acts 6:8-8:1

i)   How is Stephen described in Acts 6? Yet he is opposed.
      What can we learn about opposition to the gospel here
      - why do people oppose and what are their methods?

ii)   What are the two charges Stephen refutes (6:11, 13)?

iii) What does Stephen say is Israel's attitude to God's
      messengers in general and Moses in particular
      (7:2-43)? What characteristics of God are highlighted
      in these verses?

iv)   How had Israel blasphemed God by their attitude to
      the temple (vv. 44-50)? What had Solomon said about
      God's presence and the temple?

v)   Why did verses 51-53 anger the Sanhedrin so much?

vi)   Contrast the demeanour of Stephen and the crowd
      in verses 54-60. Who does Stephen remind you of in
      his dying? Why is it significant that the Son of Man
      stands, not sits, at God's right hand (v. 56)?

(3) Think it through
Both the Sanhedrin and Stephen claim to understand and
speak the truth. So who speaks the truth? In what ways do
each show, by their methods, words and self-discipline, who
the true preservers of God's tradition are?

(4) Live it out

i)   How are we guilty of brushing aside God's mess-
      engers?

ii)   How do we determine who speaks the truth?

iii) What are our attitudes and methods in dealing with
      a messenger of God and one who claims to be, but is
      not, a messenger of God?

iv) What does it mean for us to realise that God is the pilgrim God?

v)   Can God's messengers expect safe passage in this world?

vi) How do we see God's hidden hand at work in this section and how does it encourage us?

12

'THE STORY OF ONE: EXPANSION TO SAMARIA'

(ACTS 8:26-40)

Listening to the text

(1) The setting

Luke has been careful to give us a numerical record of the gospel's growth: three thousand in Acts 2:41, five thousand in 4:4, a rapid increase in numbers in 6:7, crowds listening to Philip in 8:6. And yet in this environment of multiple growth, Luke turns the spotlight on just one man (8:26-40). By so doing he counters our tendency to be so carried away with the corporate dimension that we forget that God deals with each person individually. Each one is precious to God.

(2) The people

Philip, one of the deacons elected in 6:5, preaches in Samaria as a result of the scattering following Stephen's martyrdom (8:4). While he is there an angel of the Lord directs him to the desert road leading from Jerusalem to Gaza. We don't know whether this fitted well with Philip's plans or whether it drove him from his comfort zone, but he started out immediately. Philip was a good choice – being a Jew from a foreign city he would have had a more open attitude to the inclusion of outsiders into the fellowship of God's people. Here is the right man on the right road, at just the right time, to meet with an important Ethiopian treasury official.

God was at work in the Ethiopian's life. He had been to Jerusalem to worship (v. 27), but being a eunuch he would not have been allowed to enter the assembly (Deut. 23:1). In all probability, he was attracted by the monotheism of Judaism and the difference it seemed to make in people's lives. Most pagan religions had little effect on life. Apart from the activity of offering to the gods, the temple rituals made no discernable difference in worshippers' everyday lives. Judaism, however, affected worshippers' lives beyond the confines of the temple: what people ate, how they used their money, when they rested etc.

The official is a thoughtful man, reading Isaiah. Philip jogs up to the chariot and breathlessly asks the man if he understands what he is reading. Needing an explanation, he invites Philip up into the chariot (v. 31). The right man, on the right road, at the right time: a man reading Isaiah 53 and needing an explanation. Luke tells us the passage, Isaiah 53:7-8, and Philip began with that passage of Scripture and explained the gospel to him.

(3) *The message*

No doubt Philip would have told him that it was Jesus who went without protest as a sheep to the slaughter, and that Jesus' life was taken in an unjust and deeply humiliating way. Philip probably rolled the scroll back to verses 4-6 of Isaiah 53, to show that it was for human transgression that

Jesus died, that we are all involved in that (Isa. 53:4), and that by his death we, the sinful, may have peace and be healed. He would have explained that all of us are disqualified from God because of sin: the eunuch also because of physical disability, but all of us because of spiritual disability. Philip's message was 'the death of the innocent for the undeserving'. And as Philip explained the gospel he would have run the scroll forward to Isaiah 53:10-12 to speak of the resurrection and vindication of Jesus. Like Peter before him with the crowds at Pentecost (2:38) he would have told the Ethiopian to repent and be baptized, as is evident from his response in verse 36. Forgiven, and having received the Holy Spirit, the Ethiopian went on his way rejoicing (v. 39 cf. Acts 2:38).

(4) The purpose

Luke includes this event to remind us that the great missionary in Acts is God himself. God chooses Philip. God directs him to the right place. God prepares the Ethiopian. The Ethiopian could have been reading many passages, but this perhaps is the most obvious Old Testament reference to the work of Christ. We should not think that God's oversight of the event ends when he brings these two men together, for he also ordains the response. 'God has granted even the Gentiles repentance unto life' (Acts 11:18) and here is one such Gentile. God is in control of the event and ordains this man's responsiveness.

Radically, the gospel changes lives. Priests in Jerusalem (6:7) and Samaritan schismatics (8:14-17) are changed profoundly, and now a new man is on his way back to Ethiopia. What changes, we might wonder, did he make to his administration of the treasury there?

From text to teaching
(1) Get the message clear
Big idea (theme)
God is the sovereign evangelist bringing about the inter-section of evangelist and seeker and ordaining the response of repentance to his message.

Big question(s) (aim)
Preaching or teaching on this passage should answer the following questions:

+ Who is Acts' greatest evangelist?
+ How does God convert one man?
+ How does God establish a divine intersection?

(2) Engage the hearer
Point of contact
In the early days of television there was a programme called 'The Naked City'. It concerned the lives of people who lived in New York City. It was one of our favourites in 1960, when my father purchased our first television, a Stromberg Carlson, seventeen inch, black and white. Each episode of 'The Naked City' ended in the same way: 'There are eight million stories in the naked city. Tonight we have seen just one of them.' Amidst the great people movements recorded by Luke that mark the growth of the early church, today we will look at just one man.

Dominant picture(s)
From a 'Google-Earth' perspective we could watch this intersection of two lives taking place. A well prepared earnest seeker meets (by chance?) a well directed and able evangelist. The seeker, a highly respected outcast of

Judaism (an up and outer) is changed profoundly, meets Jesus and goes on his way rejoicing, back to his duties in Ethiopia. The evangelist is taken away to continue his work elsewhere.

(3) Work on application
Necessary application(s)
God's heart is for the lost. A church or a Christian that ceases to be missionary, ceases to be Christian.

Refute impossible application(s)
This incident refutes the attitude that says, 'God is sovereign, let him do the work of evangelism.' When William Carey expressed his desire to serve in India, he received the response, 'Young man, sit down. When God pleases to convert the heathen he will do it without your help or mine.'

Nor does God, calling on Philip to explain the Scriptures to the Ethiopian, allow the following sentiment to remain unchallenged – 'I let my life do the talking.' The Bible knows no such thing as a silent Christian. What is on the heart will find its way to the tongue (Matt. 12:34). See where a simple question leads – 'Do you understand what you are reading?'

Possible application(s)
Am I sensitive to the intersections in my own life? As I travel on the train, bus or plane, am I looking to open up a conversation? Do I see every meeting as an opportunity? God knows where he will take the conversation!

Proclaiming the message
A preaching outline
Title: 'The Story Of One: Expansion To Samaria'
Text: Acts 8:26-40

(1)   **God directs** (8:26)
(2)   **God prepares** (8:27-28)
(3)   **The Spirit tells** (8:29)
(4)   **The question** (8:30)
(5)   **The need** (8:31)
(6)   **The passage affirms** (8:32-33)
(7)   **The response** (8:36, 38)

The great missionary in Acts is God himself.

Leading a Bible study
Title: 'The Story Of One: Expansion To Samaria'
Text: Acts 8:26-40

(1) Introduce the issues
Is life full of haphazard coincidences or divinely established intersections? Do we recognise that there are no accidents in life but that the sovereign God establishes events to lead us to Christ and then having led us to him, to make us more and more like him?

(2) Study the passage
Acts 8:26-40

i)   Do what you can to find:
           - the Gaza road on a map;
           - the place of the eunuch in God's economy;
           - and who was Candace, Queen of the Ethiopians (vv. 26-27)?

ii) The Ethiopian was not a Jew. Why then do you think he had been to Jerusalem to worship (v. 27)?

iii) How do you think Philip understood that he was being directed by the angel (vv. 26, 29)?

iv) According to verse 35, Philip evangelised the Ethiopian from Isaiah 53:7-8. What are the points Philip would have explained in response to the Ethiopian's question in verse 34?

v) Who is in charge of this evangelistic encounter?

vi) Do you think God's oversight ended before the Ethiopian's response (see 11:18)?

vii) Philip, like Peter, apparently called on the Ethiopian to 'repent and be baptised' (see 2:38). Why do you think baptism is an important companion to repentance? Why don't we give baptism the emphasis it seemed to have in the early church?

(3) *Think it through*

Are we willing to be directed like Philip and take the gospel where the Lord Jesus, the Lord of the harvest, directs us?

(4) *Live it out*

i) Do we recognise the divine intersections in our lives? The evangelistic opportunities that come our way in the train, bus, the dentist's or doctor's surgery often pass us by. Are we too silent?

ii) Do we let our lives do the talking?

iii) How are you challenged by the Scripture's link of the heart and the mouth (see Luke 6:43-45 and Rom. 10:9-10)?

iv) How can you begin conversations which God may take up and lead to opportunities for evangelism?

13

'A Surprising Conversion'

(Acts 9:1-20; 22:1-22; 26:1-32)

Listening to the text

If there is to be Gentile inclusion into God's church then someone must be the apostle to the Gentiles, and so God converts and commissions the arch-persecutor of the church, Saul of Tarsus. This is a major turning point in the narrative, and typically for such an important event, Luke records it three times. We examine the three passages together in this chapter.

(1) Saul's conversion (Acts 9:1-20)

We first meet Saul in 8:1 giving approval to Stephen's death. In Acts 9 he is on the road to Damascus, a distance of three hundred kilometres (just under two hundred miles) from Jerusalem, carrying letters of authority from the High Priest to arrest Christians in the synagogues there and return them as prisoners to Jerusalem. Saul sees that the new way and the old way cannot co-exist. If righteousness with God is by grace through faith, then it is no longer by works of obedience. To protect the old way, Saul seeks to destroy the new alternative. But God intervenes (vv. 3-6).

We are told three things that would have been remarkable for a Pharisee who knew the Scriptures:

+   a light flashed from heaven (v. 3);
+   a voice speaks (v. 4);
+   Saul is addressed by name (v. 4).

This closely parallels Moses' experience, where the bush burns, a voice addresses Moses (Exod. 3:2-4), and, as with Saul, his name is solemnly repeated. Note Jesus' use of repetition previously when addressing Simon (Luke 22:31, 'Simon, Simon...'), Jerusalem (Luke 13:34, 'O Jerusalem, Jerusalem...'), and God (Mark 15:34, 'My God, my God...'). The voice asks Saul the reason for his continuous persecution and makes it clear that this is a personal issue, 'Why do *you* persecute *me*?' Saul's response (v. 5) is to ask, 'Who are you, Lord?' The voice could have responded, 'I am God', in which case Saul could still have felt justified in persecuting the Christian church on behalf of Yahweh. But in verse 5, Jesus identifies himself and in an instant Saul realises that the crucified one lives, and that the church is the genuine people of God. Saul is then temporarily blinded and told to go to Damascus to await further instructions.

Meanwhile, Ananias has a vision and is told to go to Saul to restore his sight, since God has given Saul a vision to this effect. Saul's reputation precedes him and Ananias is reluctant (vv. 13-14). Ananias is told to go, for Saul is God's chosen instrument to take the gospel to the Gentiles. Ananias obeys and Saul is healed, filled with the Holy Spirit and baptized (vv. 17-18). At once, he begins to preach that

Jesus is the Son of God (v. 20). What a surprise for the congregation as they gathered that day!

What Saul learnt, Paul never forgot. No wonder Paul emphasises God's grace, for he had been treated by the Lord Jesus contrary to his deserving (1 Tim. 1:13-15). At the core of Paul's theology was the position of the believer 'in Christ' (Rom. 5:12-21). Saul learns here that to persecute believers is to persecute Christ himself because of the solidarity between Christ and all those who are 'in him' by faith. 'Why do you persecute me?' (v. 4)

(2) Reprise (Acts 22:1-22)

In chapter 22, Luke records Paul repeating this event before the crowd in Jerusalem. Paul addresses them respectfully as 'brothers and fathers', and in their mother tongue, Aramaic (v. 1). He relates his testimony emphasising not only his Jewishness, but the Jewishness of God's messenger Ananias (v. 12). The crowd are quite happy for him to refer to Jesus as God's righteous one and quite happy for Paul to be his witness 'to all men' (vv. 14-15), provided, of course, that means all Jewish men. The sticking point for the religious audience is verse 21: 'Go; I will send you far away to the Gentiles'.

The religious, parochial spirit is stirred. They were God's by birth, confident of their relationship with God, resistant to the inclusion of any who were not born as they were. Here is ethnic prejudice mixed with self righteousness. They had become a nation of older brothers rather than prodigal sons. They resent the free offer of that which they were working so hard to achieve and maintain. Their response to Paul lays bare their attitude to the Gentiles. They call out: 'Rid the earth of him! He's not fit to live!'

(v. 22). Comfortable, prejudiced parochialism is always the haven of the religious.

(3) Reprise (Acts 26:1-32)

The last repetition of the event is in chapter 26, where Paul appears before King Agrippa, his wife Bernice and the Roman Governor, Festus. Luke records a fuller account of Paul's commissioning in verses 16-18 than previously. The Gentiles are mentioned in verse 17 and verse 20, but this is no problem to Festus and Agrippa. Festus interrupts with the charge of insanity in verse 24.

Here Paul is confronted with the objection of the pagan, Gentile mind. The sticking point is his reference to the resurrection of the dead in verse 23. Such a fascination is also evident in Athens (17:18). Before the speech Paul has referred to this hope (vv. 7-8), and now he doesn't back down from it. The pagan mind had no place for an after-life and the thought of resurrection is therefore challenging because it refers to a reality for which they are totally unprepared.

Festus believes Paul's learning is driving him insane (v. 24). Paul responds by referring to his sober-mindedness and appeals to Agrippa's knowledge of the prophets who prove his point about the resurrection (v. 27). Paul makes it clear that his desire is to be persuasive, that all would become as he is, except of course for his prisoner status (v. 29).

From text to teaching
(1) Get the message clear
Big idea (theme)

God triumphs over the rage of his persecutor, converting Saul to be Paul, his apostle to the Gentiles.

Paul's testimony provokes the anger of the religious at Gentile inclusion and of the pagan at his confidence in the resurrection.

Big question(s) (aim)
Preaching or teaching on this passage should answer the following questions:

+ Who is in control?
+ Why do the nations rage?
+ What response can you expect to your testimony?
+ What is the biggest issue the religious mind has with the gospel?
+ What is the biggest issue the secular mind has with the gospel?

(2) Engage the hearer
Point of contact
Here is a most significant conversion. Just think that it was through understanding Paul's letter to the Romans that Luther felt 'that he had gone through open doors into paradise'. Luther's commentaries on Paul's letter to the Romans and Galatians respectively were used by God in the conversion of John and Charles Wesley. Think of Europe's culture without the Christian faith and then remember the pioneer apostle to Europe was Paul, formerly Saul the persecutor.

Dominant picture(s)
A persecutor with letters of authority and such zeal that he determinedly walked three hundred kilometres, is seen standing in a synagogue within a matter of days preaching

the divinity of the one whom he had so hated and persecuted. This is an astonishing transformation.

(3) Work on application
Necessary application(s)
The conversion of Saul, the healing of the beggar at the gate, the conversion of the Ethiopian treasurer, the resurrection of the Lord Jesus, are all evidence of God's attestation of his gospel. Christ is truly Lord. Like Saul, we need to change our conviction about Jesus' identity.

We also need to change our attitude toward commissioning for service of the gospel. For Paul, his conversion was his commissioning. Do we see our conversion as our commissioning to be servants of the gospel through which we are saved?

Refute impossible application(s)
We must refute the notion that comfortable parochialism is a haven for the Christian in a hostile world. For Christians to say that we only need to be concerned about our own church, denomination, or country is to counter God's mission to reach the lost. Parochialism is the haven of the religious mind.

We also need to beware of accepting the lie that associates unthinking closed-mindedness with the Christian mind. Not so! Acts shows that it is the secular mind that will not investigate the evidence, for fear of what it may find.

If the religious and secular minds are so dominated, then the Christian mind is to be dominated too, but by an entirely different agenda. Like Paul, we are to be dominated by a concern for the glory of God that sees his gospel taken beyond the fringe.

Possible application(s)

The opposition we face is always more irrational than the faith it attacks. We seek to reason, but in Acts the opponents of the gospel seek to silence the messengers, lock them up, or ridicule them with slander, such as accusing them of 'insanity'. Unreasonable, underhand opposition is a sign of the lack of confidence of our opponents in their own argument.

We are in the same place apologetically today as Paul was in Acts. Like him, we should seek to engage the secular mind with the historical evidence for the resurrection. All other questions about the Christian faith fall into place when you get this right.

It is sobering to note that life was not easy for Paul. He was opposed by his own and rejected, as Jesus had been. We should not imagine it will be any different for us.

Proclaiming the message
A preaching outline
Title: 'A Surprising Conversion'
Texts: Acts 9:1-20; 22:1-22; 26:1-32

(1)   **The man meets the man (9:1-20)**
  + the light (v. 3)
  + the voice (v. 4)
  + the name (v. 4)
  + why? (v. 4)
  + who? (v. 5)
  + Paul's preaching (v. 20)

(2)   **Reprise (22:1-22)**
         The sticking point – the Gentiles (vv. 21-22)

(3)   **Reprise (26:1-32)**
           The sticking point – the resurrection (vv. 23-24)

Leading a Bible study
Title: 'A Surprising Conversion'
Texts: **Acts 9:1-20; 22:1-22; 26:1-32**

(1) Introduce the issues
The conversion of one man is repeated three times in the narrative of Acts. This signals a major moment in the text for the gospel on its journey from Jerusalem to Rome. Key features of the study are the first lessons Saul learns and the nature of the opposition to him from Jews (ch. 22) and Gentiles (ch. 26).

(2) Study the passages
Acts 9:1-10
i)   How would you describe Paul's zeal as reflected in verses 1-2?
ii)   Compare Saul's experience with that of Moses in Exodus 3:1-6.
iii) What convictions does Saul have as a result of the answer in verse 5?
iv)   Why would a member of the Damascus synagogue be so surprised at Saul's preaching (v. 20)?

Acts 22:1-22
i)   How does Paul show his respect for Judaism?
ii)   Verses 17-21 are a new section in the narrative. What does this show us about God's concerns?
iii) What does the reaction of the crowd show about them (v. 22)?

iv) Why should Gentile mission be so obnoxious to the Jews?

Acts 26:12-29

i) At what point does Festus interrupt Paul? What so concerned him about what Paul was saying?

ii) Why does Paul appeal to Agrippa and his knowledge of the prophets (vv. 26-27)?

iii) Which prophets might Paul have had in mind?

iv) What does Agrippa highlight regarding Paul's ministry in verse 28?

(3) Think it through

What Saul learnt on the Damascus Road, Paul never forgot:

+ that Jesus is the resurrected Lord and Christ, the Son of God;
+ the sheer grace of God. Jesus could have swept his opponent aside but instead graciously engages him;
+ to persecute the church, those 'in Christ', is to persecute Christ himself.

(4) Live it out

i) Do you recognise that opposition to the faith is more irrational than that which it opposes?

ii) How do you encounter narrow parochialism and close-minded opposition today?

iii) What difference does it make to the way you live that you share Paul's threefold conviction from the Damascus Road?

14

'GOD'S EXPANSIVE PURPOSES'

(ACTS 10:1-11:18)

Listening to the text
(1) Overview – 'Google-Earth' perspective (10:1-48)

The 'Google-Earth' perspective of this section is fascinating. As we read, we notice that all the events dovetail perfectly. First, God prepares Cornelius. He was in the Gentile city of Caesarea, a centurion in the regiment originally made up of men from Italia. Like the other centurions we meet in the New Testament (Luke 7:2ff; 23:47) he was a man of steady mind and good reputation. But something had drawn him to Judaism for he was a God-fearer, devout and generous (vv. 2, 22). Though respected, he was technically an unclean Gentile because he was uncircumcised. Any serious Jew would not enter his house. Cornelius is given specific instructions by an angel and immediately responds (vv. 4, 8).

Meanwhile, God prepares Peter to leap an enormous barrier (vv. 9-23)! Peter, who has just told the dead Tabitha to 'get up' (9:40), and before her the paralytic Aeneas, to 'get up' (9:34), is now told in a trance: 'Get up Peter. Kill and eat' (10:13). In the vision Peter saw the heavens open and a sheet let down containing clean and unclean animals. Peter responds: 'Surely not, Lord' (v. 14). This happens three times - familiar for Peter, no doubt!

When it comes to inappropriate responses to God, Peter has plenty of 'runs on the board'! Jesus tells him where to throw his net and he responds that he has been fishing all night for nothing, so it will probably be a waste of time. It is almost as though he says:'Leave the fishing to me'(Luke 5:5). Jesus tells him Satan will sift him but he will be safe, for Jesus has prayed for him. Peter insists that Jesus shouldn't worry, he'll follow him even to death (Luke 22:31-34). When he confesses that Jesus is the Christ of God, he then tries to correct Jesus' theology of Messiahship by insisting it won't involve suffering and death (Mark 8:32). And so: 'Surely not, Lord', from Peter here, is not surprising. His reply shows that the connection between the vision and the lesson is not yet clear for him. What he has to learn is that it is no longer appropriate to apply the distinction of clean and unclean either to what you eat, or with whom you eat.

The timing is perfect - the men who left Cornelius (v. 9), now arrive (v. 19) and the Spirit tells Peter to go with them (v. 20). As Peter enters the home of Cornelius (10:23-48), his opening line in verse 28 is not designed to endear him to his audience. Nevertheless, he now seems to have made the connection: 'But God has shown me that I should not call any man impure or unclean' (v. 28). God is bringing Peter from being a man of his culture to being a man of the Kingdom. Even so, the truth revealed in the vision still hasn't entirely dawned on him, for here is the opportunistic evangelist of the earlier chapters of Acts asking: 'May I ask why you sent for me?' It hasn't yet occurred to Peter that the gospel could be for Gentiles. His blinkered understanding of Luke 24:47 is as follows: 'Repentance and forgiveness of sins will be preached in his name, to *the Jews* of all nations, beginning at Jerusalem'. That is, the gospel is for Jews only.

When Cornelius tells Peter of God's dealings with him, the penny finally drops (v. 34). Peter then preaches a three-point sermon in which he stresses:

- the life of Jesus (vv. 37-38);
- the death and resurrection of Jesus, of which he is witness (vv. 39-41);
- the coming judgment by Jesus, and that forgiveness of sin is available through him, (vv. 42-43).

In Acts 2 the Holy Spirit comes before the preaching. In Acts 8 he comes after the preaching, but here in Acts 10 he comes during the preaching, even before Peter gets to the call to repent. In verse 45 Luke describes the witnesses as 'circumcised believers', because the issue here is that the Holy Spirit has fallen on the uncircumcised, without any prerequisites of baptism or circumcision. Peter now understands, and he may well be responsible for the bracketed text at the end of Mark 7:17-19:

'After he (Jesus) had left the crowd and entered the house, his disciples asked him about this parable. "Are you so dull?" he asked. "Don't you see that nothing that enters a man from the outside can make him 'unclean'? For it doesn't go into his heart but into his stomach, and then out of his body." (In saying this, Jesus declared all foods "clean")'.

What applies to food, applies also to people. The new believers are baptized and Peter stays on with them for a few days, no doubt sharing table fellowship with them. We are not told what was on the menu, but in God's eyes it was all clean, just as all those who were present were clean because of the peace that comes through Jesus Christ (v. 36).

(2) Close-up – 'Street-level' perspective (11:1-18)

We now move from the 'Google-Earth' perspective to get the view 'on the ground' in 11:1-18. The news had reached Jerusalem before Peter did: 'You went into the house of uncircumcised men and ate with them' (v. 3). Peter tells them with great vividness what happened, noting in verse 12 that witnesses accompanied him. As he had told the Sanhedrin, so now he tells the believers that he was not going to oppose God by denying baptism to these Gentiles (v. 17). All objections are dropped and they praised God: 'So then, God has granted even the Gentiles repentance unto life' (v. 18).

The gospel to the Gentiles is an important turning point, and Luke underlines its importance by reporting it three times: in chapters 10 and 11, and then again in 15:7-11. It is an interesting event and Peter's involvement in it is a little puzzling. Peter tells the believers in 11:5: 'I was in the city of Joppa praying...' That's true, but Luke has already told us three times where he was, at Simon the tanner's house (9:43; 10:6, 32). Tanning was considered an unclean activity because it involved handling unclean carcasses. There is some evidence that tanners were forbidden to enter Jerusalem. So here is Peter in an unclean Jew's house, receiving a vision about clean and unclean food. Once again we see Luke showing people 'warts and all' – in this case providing another example of Peter's humanness. He was happy enough to accept hospitality from an unclean Jew, but to do so from an unclean Gentile was unthinkable. It required a vision to change his prejudice. The best of men are men at best!

From text to teaching
(1) *Get the message clear*
Big Idea (theme)
God leads the church to hurdle its prejudices so that his gospel reaches all peoples.

Big question(s) (aim)
Preaching or teaching on this passage should answer the following questions:

+ Who is the gospel for?
+ How wide is God's missionary purpose?
+ What is God's purpose for the nations?

(2) *Engage the hearer*
Point of contact
I find self-help television shows quite annoying. In cooking programmes, the chef's dishes always work out so well. All the ingredients are always perfectly chopped and precisely weighed. A handyman on one of these self-help shows recently constructed 'a box on castors' - a 'simple storage solution', he called it. He had all the tools to hand, and the job was done perfectly in the ten minutes between ad breaks.

It never works like that for me. My father taught me that the best tool in the tool box is the telephone – call the builder, or the plumber, or the handyman, he said!

In Acts 10-11 we see God's careful oversight. He needs no help or advice; he is a providential Father who will bring his plan to perfect fulfilment. 'It must happen', he says, and it does. Under his oversight all the pieces of the puzzle fit together perfectly.

Dominant picture(s)
One of the striking things about this event is the way all pieces fit together. Cornelius' men set out and arrive just at the right moment. As Peter is thinking about his vision the Spirit prompts him to go and meet with the men.

It is wonderful to see that when the Holy Spirit is given to 'the unclean', 'the clean' rejoice in all that God has done.

(3) *Work on application*
Necessary application(s)
God directs his church by direct speech and visions to press beyond the fringe of prejudice. The gospel is for 'up-and-outers' like Cornelius, the Ethiopian, and the Roman proconsul in chapter 13, and for 'down-and-outers' like the Philippian jailer. It is for circumcised and uncircumcised, for Africans and Europeans, for Jews, Gentiles and God-fearers. God's purpose is expansive. All of us need the peace which only Jesus Christ can give (10:36).

Refute impossible application(s)
In Christian circles you might occasionally hear it said (though in many more cases it will be silently believed) that openly sinful people need forgiveness through Jesus but respectable people don't. On the other hand, some swing the pendulum the other way and say that we should not try and reach out to unclean people who will change the look

of our church, or people who will try to change the way we do things. Both attitudes are refuted by God's expansive heart for all the lost. 'Up-and-outer', the 'mid-and-outer', the 'down-and-outer' - God's gospel is for them all!

Possible application(s)

God continues to show his concern for the salvation of the lost. How do we account for the enthusiasm and excitement of believers who have a burden to work long term in areas of the world which are insecure and just plain hard? Yet not only do they go, but they go willingly and excitedly. Where does such conviction come from? From the expansive God who still directs his church to press beyond the fringe.

Also note that as God-fearing, good and respectable as Cornelius was, he was not right with God. He did not have the 'peace through Jesus Christ' and needed to hear the gospel and be forgiven. We must never let our evangelistic zeal be blinded by the seeming goodness and respectability of the person we are seeking to reach. All people need Jesus, whatever state they are in.

Proclaiming the message

A preaching outline

Title: **'God's Expansive Purposes'**

Text: **Acts 10:1-11:18**

(1) **'Google-Earth' perspective** (10:1-48)
  + Cornelius prepared (10:1-8)
  + Peter prepared (10:9-23)
  + Peter preaches at Cornelius' home (10:23-48)

(2) **'Street-level' perspective** (11:1-18)
  + Peter defends his actions in Jerusalem (11:1-18)

Leading a Bible study
Title: **'God's Expansive Purposes'**
Text: **Acts 10:1-11:18**

(1) Introduce the issues
i)   Do we have friends and family whom we think would not be interested in any way in the Christian faith?
ii) God's purposes are expansive; no one is off limits to him. Are you prepared to believe this could even include these people? What makes this difficult to believe?

(2) Study the passage
Acts 10:1 – 11:18
i)   What reputation did Cornelius have (10:1-2)?
ii) Why was the sheet with clean and unclean animals and the command to eat them such a shock for Peter? (see Lev. 11)
iii) What was the lesson God was teaching Peter and when do you think he learned it?
iv) We are told in 9:43; 10:6; 10:32 where Peter was living. Why is it significant he should receive *such a vision* in *such a house*?
v)   From 10:34-43, how would you summarise Peter's address?
vi) Why do you believe the Holy Spirit is given here before Peter concludes his message?
vii) What is the accusation made against Peter by the brethren at Jerusalem (v. 3)?
viii) How does Peter defend himself (vv. 4-17)?
ix) What is the response of the objectors and how do they describe the Gentile experience (v. 18)?

(3) *Think it through*

Every potential barrier to the gospel's movement from Jerusalem to Rome is demolished by God. Cornelius is prepared to receive the gospel. Peter, by means of a three-fold vision, is prepared to take the gospel and communicate it to an 'unclean' Gentile. The church in Jerusalem is prepared for the inclusion of Gentiles into its ranks.

i) In what ways do people today need such preparation for the reception of the gospel, its communication and their inclusion?

ii) What response does each need call for from us?

(4) *Live it out*

i) Do we believe that people need to earn the right to receive the gospel?

ii) What changes do we look for in people to fit them for being an acceptable part of our fellowship?

iii) Do we resent God's free offer of the gospel and gracious acceptance of people who don't deserve either?

iv) As fine a man as Cornelius was - generous, God-fearing, highly respected - he nevertheless needed the peace that comes through Jesus Christ. Are there people you are tempted to believe may not need to hear the gospel?

v) How must our attitudes change in the light of these Scriptures?

15

'THE HIDDEN HAND AT WORK'

(ACTS 12:1-25)

Listening to the text

(1) Background and setting

The days couldn't be much darker than they are in Acts 12. There was something loathsome about the Herodian kings, successors of Herod the Great, who had sought to have Jesus killed, as a baby, because he viewed him as a threat to the throne. His descendants continued to be puppet kings in the Roman Empire and followed in their grandfather's footsteps. They were men given to political expediency, a lack of integrity and no compassion. This Herod is no exception. He soon discovers that the way to keep the Jews onside is to persecute Christians. And so he has James, one of the sons of Zebedee, put to death, and seizes Peter for the same purpose.

James and Peter were, with John, part of the 'inner-circle' of Jesus' disciples. They were at the transfiguration (Luke 9:28-36) and the raising of the dead girl, Jairus' daughter (Luke 8:51). James is the first martyr of the twelve.

Yet Luke devotes just a single verse to his martyrdom; literally 'killed, James the brother of John' (the only detail given in the instrumental dative case, 'with the sword', implying that he was probably decapitated). The contrast with Stephen's martyrdom is marked, with Luke's coverage running to seventy-five verses, even though Stephen is not an apostle, let alone part of an 'inner-circle' of apostles [see chapter 11 – 'The Church's First Martyr' (Acts 6:8-8:1)]. Luke doesn't comment directly, but by the extent of the coverage shows where his interest lies. The death of Stephen was a catalyst for the move of the gospel out of Jerusalem, Judea, and into Samaria. James' death, by contrast, has no discernible effect on the gospel's movement, so is covered in one brief verse.

(2) The praying church

Things look dark: James is dead, Peter is under arrest. However, Luke provides a ray of hope in verse 5: '...but the church was earnestly praying to God for him'. Here Luke is contrasting the political authority of Herod with God's sovereign control. The chapter begins well for Herod, with the Jews onside and the Christian leadership contained, but the church was praying! Luke emphasises the extent of Herod's security arrangements to guard Peter: squads of soldiers (v. 4); soldiers, chains and sentries (v. 6); two lines of guards and an iron gate (v. 10). But the church was praying.

What happens? Peter is asleep and is told by an angel to 'get up' (v. 7 [similar to 10:13]). He is told to get dressed, and as he passes by the guards, he does not realise what is happening. Previously, Peter might have objected to his instructions: 'Surely not, Lord,' but this time he obeys without question. Peter is learning! In 10:34 he comments: 'I now realise how true it is...' And here again in 12:11, he expresses his confidence in God's sovereign control: 'Now I know without a doubt'. How was he set free? Because the church was earnestly praying to God for him.

Again Luke doesn't paint an idealistic picture of the church. He shows us that their prayer was effective, but imperfect. Peter goes to the house of Mary where the church is meeting to pray for him (v. 12). When the servant girl, Rhoda, recognises his voice at the gate, she excitedly runs inside to tell everyone of Peter's release. These are the people who have been praying earnestly for Peter. Did they believe God would release him? Evidently not, for they say she's either out of her mind, or has seen Peter's angel (v. 15). Meanwhile, Peter keeps knocking! They open the door and are astonished to see him (v. 16). Their prayers are answered, but the pray-ers themselves find it unbelievable. Apparently, God has answered unbelieving prayer!

Herod's ruthlessness is shown in his summary execution of the soldiers who had guarded Peter (v. 19). He had fallen out of relationship with the people of Tyre and Sidon and had cut off their food supplies. This accounts for their response to his speech in verse 22. Why else would seemingly rational people respond to a political speech by proclaiming: "This is the voice of a god, not of a man"? Herod accepted praise due to God, and immediately the angel who struck Peter awake, strikes Herod down (v. 23). Herod, who had denied food to Tyre and Sidon, himself becomes food for worms and dies. And the result of God's removal of this arch-protagonist who opposed the gospel? 'But the Word of God continued to increase and spread' (v. 24). A chapter which had begun so well for Herod, and looked so dark for the church (the death of the apostle James and the imprisonment of the apostle Peter), ends with the deliverance of Peter, the death of Herod, the triumph of the Word, and the beginning of a mission to the Gentiles, ready to press out beyond the fringe to the ends of the earth (v. 25). Such radical reversal is indicative of the unstoppable progress of the gospel and a great encouragement!

From text to teaching
(1) Get the message clear
Big idea (theme)
God's ultimate end is to glorify himself through the progress of the gospel. He is a loving, caring shepherd of his sheep and deals decisively with those who oppose the gospel.

Big question(s) (aim)
Preaching or teaching on this passage should answer the following questions:

+ Who rules?
+ Why does God let one die and release another?
+ What is God's ultimate purpose?
+ What is the impact of a praying church?
+ How does God deal with those who oppose the gospel?

(2) Engage the hearer
Point of contact
'We've lost her'; 'The news is not good'; or 'I am sorry to have to inform you' are statements we often hear. Do we have anything to say in the light of bad news? The world's consolations, well intentioned as they may be, are empty, for example: 'She has had a good innings', or 'What will be, will be'. Do we have anything more substantial to say? In Acts 12, the church is faced with dark days. What is their response?

Dominant picture(s)

There is a strong contrast between the political power wielded by Herod and the sovereign supernatural power of God. It may look and feel like Herod is calling the shots, but in reality God is absolutely in control. The contrast between human and divine power is seen most powerfully in Herod's wormy death, contrasted with the vitality of the Word of God and its messengers.

(3) Work on application

Necessary application(s)

God is to be trusted, no matter how dark things appear. God will always act to glorify his name and advance his gospel. Calm, secure trust in him must be our response in all situations. His 'hidden hand' is at work.

When facing difficulty and opposition, the church's response must be to pray.

We are safe and secure until our work on earth for the gospel is complete. Paul is assured of this by God in Acts 18:10. God still had work for Peter to do. He was to be a vital witness before the Jerusalem Council in chapter 15. James' ministry is over, so God takes him home. 'God buries his messengers, but not his message'. God's greater purpose than our safety on earth is his glory through the fulfilment of his plans. His messengers come and go, and then enter into their eternal reward, but God's gospel moves on beyond the fringe.

Refute impossible application(s)

The execution of James, and the imprisonment of Peter, powerfully exposes the false teaching of a prosperity gospel. To declare that 'God has no greater purpose than the earthly status, health and wealth of those who are his' is worldly and blind.

Similarly, the sovereign rule of God seen in this chapter rules out any view that life is random, luck rules, and we take our chances, hoping that things will turn out right. God's hand may be hidden, but it is a powerful, all-controlling hand, acting from a heart of love. All glory is to be to God alone.

Possible application(s)
Do I recognise my perfect safety until my work is done for the Lord Jesus? God's providence is perfect; he is a careful shepherd of his sheep.

Reflecting on Psalm 116:15: 'Precious in the sight of the Lord is the death of his saints', Spurgeon writes: 'They shall not die prematurely, they shall be immortal till the work is done; and when their time comes to die then their deaths shall be precious. The Lord watches over their dying beds, smoothes their pillows, sustains their hearts, receives their soul.'

Do I treat prayer as a technique for getting what I want? Prayer is about relationship, and God is not bound by our imperfections. We may say things wrongly or say things without sufficient belief, but God loves to hear his people pray and is well able to do immeasurably more than we can ask or imagine (Eph. 3:20).

Do I recognise that God is jealous for the affection and devotion of his people? His majesty and glory is to be recognised by the self effacing humility of his people. He esteems the one who is humble and contrite and who trembles at his word (Isa. 66:2).

Proclaiming the message
A preaching outline
Title: 'The Hidden Hand At Work'
Text: Acts 12:1-25

(1) **Dark days for the church** (vv. 1-5)
  ✦   James martyred (vv. 1-2)
  ✦   Peter imprisoned (vv. 3-4)
  ✦   Earnest prayer (v. 5)

(2) **God's sovereignty** (vv. 6-25)
  ✦   Peter miraculously released (vv. 6-11)
  ✦   Prayer effective, but imperfect (vv. 12-19a)
  ✦   Removal of Herod (vv. 19b-23)
  ✦   The Word spreads (vv. 24-25)

Leading a Bible study
Title: 'The Hidden Hand At Work'
Text: Acts 12:1-25

(1) Introduce the issues
Here is a chapter of severe setbacks for the life of the church, as well as supernatural reversals of fortune. The chapter passes through the darkness of persecution and imprisonment, before recounting the release of Peter from prison, and the removal of Herod. The end result is the increase in the Word and the progress of the gospel. Can we trust that the hidden hand of God is at work even in dark days?

(2) Study the passage

Acts 12:1-25

i)   What motivated Herod to kill James and imprison Peter?

ii) To what extraordinary lengths did Herod go to ensure Peter's secure imprisonment?

iii) Why is verse 5 key?

iv) What do verses 13-16 tell us about the quality of the church's prayer?

v)   Why do you think Peter was miraculously rescued while James was not?

vi) What sort of a man was Herod and why did he deserve his end?

vii) Why do verses 23 and 24 provide such a vivid contrast?

viii) Why is verse 25 such a significant conclusion to the chapter?

ix) What does the chapter teach us about God and prayer (consider also Eph. 3:20)?

(3) Think it through

In this chapter we see evidence of God's sovereign power and of his jealousy. God is jealous for the glory due to his name. How do both these characteristics of God challenge the way we live and minister in his name?

(4) Live it out

i)   Dark days come to all of us. How do we find reassurance from this chapter?

ii) Think of God's activity in the life of Herod, James, Peter and the praying church at Mary's home. Try to imagine how each of these characters, and Rhoda representing the church, might describe the events of the chapter. Whose testimony do you particularly relate to?

iii) Having studied this chapter, what fruit should it produce in our lives?

16

'OUR MOTHER CHURCH'

(ACTS 11:19-30; 13:1-3)

Listening to the text

This section links to the past and prepares for the future growth of the Gentile church. Until now, we have read of Philip's evangelistic encounter with the God-fearing Gentile Ethiopian, and Peter's encounter with the God-fearing Gentile Cornelius. Now we have the account of the birth and growth of a large Gentile church.

(1) The beginning of the church

Acts 11:19 takes us back to Acts 8:1, the scattering of believers as a result of the persecution related to Stephen's martyrdom. We are reintroduced to Barnabas and reminded of his character and his interest in Saul (see 9:27). Saul therefore has his first experience of ministry to the Gentiles during the twelve months he is in Antioch (11:26).

In response to the prophecy of Agabus, a collection is taken for the church in Judea (11:27-30). This gift, helpful in its own right, was also symbolically important. It underlined the link between the church in Antioch and the mother church in Jerusalem, a connection already made apparent by the elders' authority in appointing Barnabas. The Gentile church recognised their indebtedness to the church from which the gospel and their pastor had come. The Gentile believers were different from the Jewish believers, but this collection represented the honouring of their unity. They were different, but part of the one fellowship in unity with Jesus Christ.

The gift was also the means of taking Barnabas and Saul to Jerusalem, so that Saul had the opportunity to strengthen the links of the Jewish church to his Gentile mission. This is probably the visit Paul refers to in Galatians 2:1: 'Fourteen years later I went up again to Jerusalem, this time with Barnabas'.

(2) *The scattering*
Those scattered by the persecution travelled from Jerusalem to the north. They were Jews who had lived outside Jerusalem but they shared the previous reluctance of Peter, shown in their speaking the gospel only to fellow Jews. However, some gospelled 'Greeks also'. The emphasis of their message was that Jesus Christ is Lord, similar to Peter's emphasis in Acts 10:36: '...Jesus Christ, who is Lord of all'. They preached the Lordship of Jesus (v. 20), and a great number turned to the Lord. Luke therefore concludes that the Lord's hand was with them (v. 21). Three times Luke tells us of the great response (vv. 21, 24, 26). While all of this is a result of God's hand at work, God's hand does not work in isolation. He uses the human instrument. In this case the believers from Cyprus and Cyrene were the

church planters (v. 20). Barnabas (v. 24), and Barnabas and Saul (v. 26) were the church establishers.

Jesus had told the disciples that their ministry was always a 'co-ministry'. It was always the Holy Spirit working through the church (John 15:26-27). So it is here - God's hand working through Barnabas, Saul and the original church planters, resulting in a great response.

God's purpose is always more expansive than that recognised by the church. Think of the Father's response to the Son in Psalm 2:8: 'Ask of me, and I will make the nations your inheritance, the ends of the earth your possession'. Jesus Christ is Lord of all and all need to be given the opportunity of recognising his Lordship. No one is ever to be considered 'off-limits'.

(3) The establishment of the church

The Jerusalem church was interested and involved with the development of this new work and they make the sensitive appointment of Barnabas to oversee the congregation at Antioch. In Acts 11:18 they had rejoiced that 'God had granted even the Gentiles repentance unto life'. They could have appointed a man who saw the circumcision of the new believers in Antioch as his first priority.

Barnabas, of course, was not an apostle, but the Antiochene believers, having received the gospel were Christians. What they needed was encouragement. And Barnabas, true to his reputation, did exactly that, encouraging them 'to remain true to the Lord with all their hearts' (v. 23). The description of Barnabas in 11:24 is similar to the other glimpses we have of him in Acts (4:36-37; 9:27; 15:37).

Barnabas saw evidence of the grace of God at work (v. 23) in the Antiochene believers' repentance and in their faith (v. 21). There was no vestige of the resentment of the 'elder brother' about him. He rejoiced and encouraged them to remain wholeheartedly true (v. 23).

But the ongoing growth in the number of believers meant that he needed help. He had not forgotten Saul, and so he made the journey to Tarsus (one hundred and sixty kilometres / one hundred miles) to seek him out. And so they served together for twelve months at Antioch. Barnabas' concern was that the Antiochenes become well established in the faith. This emphasis on 'establishment' is seen again in Acts 14:21-23, when the missionaries return, 'strengthening the disciples and encouraging them' and appointing elders. Acts 20 tells us that the role of the elder was to shepherd God's flock and 'proclaim to you the whole will of God' (Acts 20:27).

This strong emphasis on establishment continued in the early church, so that by AD 150, a book entitled *The Didache* appeared as a manual for establishing believers in the faith. It covered such topics as advice for living the Christian life, relating to leaders in the church, understanding the sacraments and prayer, discerning the Word of God and its counterfeit, the importance of church, relating to the government and the Christian hope. How this stands in stark contrast to our day, when there is little attention given to the curriculum which should be covered by new believers! The triune God, grace, justification, assurance, the Holy Spirit in the believer's life, the church, the return of Christ, the world and our responsibilities are all areas in which new believers need to receive systematic instruction.

Here then is the apostle, commissioned by God for Gentile work, having his first taste of ministry to the

Gentile church, to fulfil, in part, Acts 9:15: '...to carry my name before the Gentiles.'

(4) The life of the church

Great numbers of people were thus taught the truth. What were they taught? No doubt 'the whole will of God' (Acts 20:27). This surely is the key. Everything this church is and does comes back to God's grace and the fact that they were well-established in the truth. This establishment was carried out over an intensive twelve month period.

After Rome and Alexandria, Josephus rates Antioch the third city in the empire in terms of population and prosperity (*The Wars of the Jews*, Book 3:2:4). This is a strategic centre, the sending post for the Gentile mission, and like all the churches reached in Acts, the apostles show their concern to see the work well established.

Antiochenes, apparently, had a reputation for giving nicknames (see A.C. Gaebelein *Commentary on Acts*, p. 216), and it's here that believers are called 'Christians' for the first time (v. 26). This title will be repeated in Acts 26:28. The point is that Christians are now recognised as a large enough group to warrant identification in their own right. Until now, the Christians had probably been regarded as a sect of Judaism. Now they are seen as a group having their own separate identity, followers of Jesus the Messiah.

The nickname is written in Greek, having a Latin adjectival form (*-ianis*) and refers to a Hebrew concept, Christ, the anointed one. Luke thus reminds us of the universal dimension of the Lordship of Christ - he is for Jews, Greeks and Romans, the Lord of us all. This does not mean that the church saw itself as separated from Judaism; they probably still believed that they were part of the new

Israel of God, and their ongoing links to Jerusalem is evidence of that thinking.

Prophets are active in the church in fulfilment of Joel's prophecy, quoted in Acts 2:17-18 (esv):

> 'And in the last days it shall be, God declares, that I will pour out my Spirit on all flesh, and your sons and your daughters shall prophesy, and your young men shall see visions, and your old men shall dream dreams; even on my male servants and female servants in those days I will pour out my Spirit, and they shall prophesy.'

Agabus, through the Spirit, predicted a severe famine in the Roman world in the time of the emperor Claudius (ad 41-54) (Agabus' prophecy can be dated to around ad 44). Josephus refers to such a famine (*Antiquities* 3.15.3). Again, demonstrating the principles seen in earlier acts of generosity (2:45; 4:34), the Gentile Christians of Antioch provide help for those in Judea, 'each according to his ability' (11:29). There are links here with the Joseph narrative (referred to by Stephen in Acts 7:11-16) when Joseph helped his family. Here, apparently, the church in Antioch, recognising its superior prosperity to Judea, gladly shares of that prosperity to relieve the effects of a famine which had not yet taken place. The prophetic activity, the church's respect for it and generous response to it, are further evidence of the grace of God and of God's hand being at work among them.

(5) A growing church
Barnabas and Saul take the collection to Jerusalem and return to Antioch with Mark (12:25). The church continues

to grow and so does the leadership team. A church of such diversity is reflected in the variety of its leaders, now numbering five (13:1-5). They are Barnabas (a Levite from Cyprus), Simeon (a black African from Niger), Lucius of Cyrene (a North African), Manaen (something of an aristocrat having been raised in the household of Herod) and Saul, a well educated Pharisee from Tarsus. Barnabas is mentioned first, Saul last. The Jewish name Saul soon changes to the Graeco-Roman Paul (13:9), more appropriate for one who will carry the gospel to the Gentiles. Soon Paul is to be listed before Barnabas (13:42, 50; 14:1, 3). But at the Jerusalem Council in chapter 15, Peter takes priority, and again Barnabas precedes Paul, who is given a somewhat lower profile (15:7, 12, 22, 25). Paul is something of an outsider to the Christian church in Jerusalem. It was while the five Antiochene leaders were worshipping and fasting that the Holy Spirit spoke clearly to them. In Luke 5:35 Jesus makes it clear that such fasting is appropriate after the bridegroom has gone, and the church probably saw fasting as a means of preparing to hear the guiding voice of God.

The work of Barnabas and Saul and the Gentile mission is not of human origin. It is God's work, God's plan, God's call to them, and they are to be set apart for the work by the Holy Spirit (13:2). (Paul uses similar words in Romans 1:1 to describe his commission). In verse 3, there is further fasting and prayer before the three remaining leaders commission Barnabas and Saul and send them off through the laying on of hands. Luke reminds us, that though commissioned by human hands, it was the Holy Spirit who sent them on their way (13:4).

Here is a well-taught church showing clear evidence of God's grace in its repentance and faith. But it also shows a sensitive, careful hearing of the prophetic word, either through a human prophet, Agabus, or directly from the Holy Spirit. No doubt Paul would have told them, as he had the Thessalonians: 'Do not put out the Spirit's fire; do not treat prophecies with contempt. Test everything' (1 Thess. 5:19-21). In each case, the response of the church showed how seriously they took the direction of God, sharing their wealth with their mother church in its need, and then being willing to send off their two most senior pastors to continue the work of mission. What a challenge they are to the mindset that would keep the best for itself and let God have the rest.

The clear emphasis here is on the expansive purpose of God. 'The Holy Spirit said' (13:2) is one example of the twenty-two direct voices of God in the text of Acts. The majority of these, like this one, remind the church to press out beyond the fringe. The following examples are notable:

+ 'Go, stand in the temple courts…and tell the people the full message of this new life' (5:20).
+ 'Go south to the road – the desert road…' (8:26).
+ 'Go! This man is my chosen instrument to carry my name before the Gentiles…' (9:15).
+ 'Simon, three men are looking for you. So get up and go downstairs. Do not hesitate to go with them, for I have sent them' (10:20).
+ "Set apart for me Barnabas and Saul for the work to which I have called them" (Acts 13:2).
+ 'Come over to Macedonia and help us' (16:9).
+ 'For I am with you, and no-one is going to attack you and harm you, because I have many people in this city' (Acts 18:10).

What do these direct words from God tell us about him?

> *Can we, whose souls are lighted*
> *With wisdom from on high,*
> *Can we to men benighted*
> *The lamp of life deny?*
> *Salvation! O Salvation!*
> *The joyful sound proclaim,*
> *Till each remotest nation*
> *Has learnt Messiah's name.*
>   (Reginald Heber)

From text to teaching

(1) Get the message clear

Big idea (theme)

God's purpose is to see his church well established and reaching beyond the fringe, proclaiming his grace so that previously unreached Gentiles turn to the Lord and believe.

Big question(s) (aim)

Preaching or teaching on this passage should answer the following questions:

- ✦ Where is God at work?
- ✦ How does God work?
- ✦ What is the evidence of God's grace?
- ✦ What is the church to be like?
- ✦ What are God's fellow-workers to be like?

(2) Engage the hearer

Point of contact

In his retirement my father developed an interest in genealogy. Who were our forebears, where had they come from, what had they done in life, what sort of people were they? Was there any link to the famous Captain James Cook who discovered Australia? To be interested in our spiritual genealogy is a healthy thing. Here is our mother church, the first church of Gentiles. How far have we moved from her?

Dominant picture(s)
People are familiar with the notion that for the abstract to be seen, it must be evidenced in the concrete. So the link can be made to how God's grace is seen – in people who were ignorant, apathetic, calloused pagans, now turning their back on all that and recognising the Lordship of Jesus Christ in all of life. It is the concrete evidence of the abstract.

(3) Work on application
Necessary application(s)
The church of God is to be well established and then, under God's direction, press out with the gospel of grace to the next street, village, city and country.

Refute impossible application(s)
Some have understood the mission God has given the church but have then gone on to say that the church should *just* be concerned for evangelism, and does not need to take establishment of new believers seriously. The missionary-minded church at Antioch refutes this.

We should note that God's heart is always to press beyond the fringe, but the people he uses to lead this are well-established in their understanding of the gospel of his grace. This is a clear emphasis of apostolic ministry, not only here, but in Acts 14:21-25; 15:22, 41; 16:1-5;

20:1-6, and in Paul's rehearsal of his strategy for ministry in Acts 20:13-38. Superficial Christ-ian knowledge leads to superficial evangelism, preaching a pale counterfeit of the gospel of grace.

The key to the health of the church of Antioch was God's hand of blessing on Barnabas and Saul as they taught the new believers for a whole year. Growth in knowledge is not to be seen as an alternative to generous and sacrificial outreach, but the foundation for such outreach.

Possible application(s)
+ Do I rejoice in every evidence of God's grace at work in the lives of people, and are my responses to grace always generous?
+ Do I keep the best and share the rest?
+ Does our church see its role as establishing people well in God's grace and then being a clearing house, seeing them move out beyond the fringe?
+ When was I last involved in a discipling, mentoring, establishing ministry?

Proclaiming the message
A preaching outline
Title: **'Our Mother Church'**
Texts: **Acts 11:19-30; 13:1-3**

(1) **The beginning of the church** (11:19-21)

(2) **The establishment of the church**
+ Barnabas (11:22-24)
+ Barnabas and Saul (11:25-26)

(3) **The life of the church**
  ✦   Sensitive to the voice of God
  ✦   Generous response (11:27-30)
  ✦   Sensitive to the voice of God
  ✦   Generous response (13:1-3)

Leading a Bible study
Title: **'Our Mother Church'**
Texts: **Acts 11:19-30; 13:1-3**

(1) Introduce the issues
For those of us who are non-Jewish Christians, here is our mother church. Luke gives a full description of the proto-Jewish-Christian community in Jerusalem (Acts 2).

(2) Study the passages
Acts 11:19-30; 13:1-3

i)   Why do you think those scattered in 8:1 and 11:19 told the gospel only to Jews? Why was it such a big step to share the gospel with Greeks also (v. 20)?

ii)   According to verse 20, what in particular did they share with the Greeks (see Acts 10:36)?

iii)   In Acts 11:18, 16:14 and here in Acts 11:21, Luke records God's actions in bringing people to faith in Christ. Does the Lord work independently of human activity?

iv)   Why was the choice of Barnabas by the Jerusalem elders such a sensitive one?

v)   How does Luke summarise the ministry of Barnabas (vv. 23-24)?

vi)   Barnabas had previously sponsored Saul in Jerusalem (9:27). Why does he seek Saul out now and what is the special significance of this twelve month ministry for Saul (see Acts 9:15)?

vii) What characteristics of the early church's life are shown in verse 27-30? Why are they like this?

viii) What can we learn about the church at Antioch from the make-up of its leaders listed in 13:1?

ix) What does Luke emphasise here and in verse 4 about the ministry of Barnabas and Saul?

x) In terms of its response to God's Word, what similar characteristic of the church is evident here in 13:1-3, as in 11:27-30?

(3) *Think it through*

Being well established in grace, carefully hearing the Word of God, together with a generous, open-handed response to that Word - how much are these qualities evident in our church life?

(4) *Live it out*

Luke emphasises that the gospel's expansion is the purpose of God, but not at the expense of seeing believers well established in the gospel. It is God's plan that the gospel should come to Antioch, that large numbers of people should come to faith and be established in grace, and that the church should send out its founding leadership to take the gospel to other regions. How will I/we partner God's hand at work today, his hand which acts from his heart for the lost world?

SERIES THREE:

The Unstoppable Gospel!

Acts 13:4-28:31

17

'WHAT'S IN A NAME'

(ACTS 13:4-14:28)

Listening to the text

Acts is great literature. Great literature has many layers of subtle meaning and Acts is no exception. One of the features of Luke's reporting of the first missionary journey is the way he uses names to provide stress, irony, contrast and comparison. We see it in the change in order of Barnabas and Saul to Paul and Barnabas; in the change of name from Saul to Paul; in the contrast of Saul/Paul to King Saul; in the comparison of Sergius Paulus and Paul and in the contrast of Bar-Jesus with Jesus.

There are also close parallels between Paul and the early ministry of Jesus, showing the solidarity of Jesus with one of his primary representatives in Acts. There are also close parallels to Peter's ministry, showing that Paul is an apostle of equal standing with Peter. The divided response to Paul's gospel ministry is another feature of this first missionary journey.

(1) Mission in Cyprus (Acts 13:4-12)

It is fitting that Barnabas and Saul should begin their tour moving through Cyprus, the home of Barnabas. They move through the island east to west, from Salamis to Paphos. Though sent by a Gentile church and commissioned by God for Gentile mission, they begin in the synagogue. They do this not only because God had ordained the Jews to be the first to receive his words (Rom. 3:1-2), and therefore also the gospel ('first for the Jew' as Paul says in Rom. 1:16), but also because Paul and Barnabas know that the synagogues, containing Jews and God-fearers, are fertile ground for ministry.

In Paphos they contact a Jewish sorcerer who was an adviser to the local Roman representative – a proconsul, an appointment of the Roman Senate. Luke tells us these men's names. The sorcerer's name, Bar-Jesus, means literally 'son of Jesus' (v. 6). Luke also tells us his Greek name, Elymas (v. 8), to emphasise his heretical character as a Jew using a Greek name, and to distance him from Christ Jesus whose solemn name he bears. Saul distances himself from this sorcerer straight away. Because of his opposition, Saul recognises that Bar-Jesus' deceit and trickery identify him not with Jesus, but as one in kinship with the Devil, the father of lies (John 8:44). The temporary blindness that comes upon Elymas (v. 11) is the first sign God does through Paul. It is a declaration of judgment, very much like Saul's own experience. We are not told whether or not, as in Paul's case, the man came to believe.

Sergius Paulus, by contrast, is an intelligent man (v. 7) – and one wonders why he bothered with Bar-Jesus. Seeing what happened to his adviser and having heard the Word of God, he believes (v. 12). At this point Luke switches from using Saul's Hebrew name and begins using his Greek name, Paul (v. 9). Paul is a more fitting name given his empire-wide ministry. The name change also suggests a close connection between the senatorial representative, Sergius Paulus, and God's representative, Paul. Maybe Luke wants to show Paul's equal footing with these Roman provincial leaders.

(2) Mission in Pisidian Antioch (Acts 13:13–52)

The party, now minus John Mark, move on to Pisidian Antioch and visit the synagogue. Paul is now clearly the spokesman (13:16) and his name precedes Barnabas' in 13:46 and 13:50. There is no evidence of competition between the two; the name order simply reflects the reality of giftedness and leadership. Back in Jerusalem, where he is better known, Barnabas precedes Paul; but generally from here onwards, Paul is mentioned first. As someone insightfully observed: 'It takes more grace than I can tell you to play the second fiddle well'.

Having heard Stephen's speech, Paul now speaks very much like him. Paul's historic overview is briefer than Stephen's and provides the only reference in Acts to his namesake, King Saul (vv. 21-22). Saul's reign is remembered for his lack of regard for God's Word. By contrast, Paul will lead fruitfully because of his zeal for God's Word.

Paul says that God has sent the Son of David, the saviour Jesus, and that through Jesus salvation is now available for Jews and God-fearing Gentiles (vv. 16-26). This Jesus was rejected by his own, killed, raised from the dead by God, and then seen by many witnesses (vv. 27-31).

The Sanhedrin had not allowed Stephen to get this far. Paul uses the opportunity to emphasise the resurrection of Jesus. He says this is the fulfilment of Psalm 2, God the

Father's promise not to David – for he died and decayed – but to his Son, Jesus. It follows that Jesus is the Son of the Father (v. 33); that Jesus is the recipient of the blessings of rule and inheritance promised to David (v. 34); and that the resurrected Jesus will never see decay (v. 35). The resurrection of Jesus is therefore the guarantee of salvation and of the forgiveness of sins.

The offer of forgiveness is made through faith in Jesus (v. 38). One would expect the author of Galatians and Romans to speak as he does in verse 39. The stress here is that righteousness and forgiveness are found in this man. It is through this man that forgiveness of sin is announced (v. 39). It is by this man that everyone who believes is justified (v. 39). Paul says that the law was incomplete (vv. 32-33) and cannot save (v. 39). It is by faith in this man, rather than by punctilious legal obedience, that salvation (vv. 23, 26), good news (v. 32), and forgiveness of sin (vv. 38, 39) have come.

When good news is preached to a Jewish audience there is always a note of warning. The Synagogue is warned against fulfiling the prophecy that describes them as those who would scoff and not believe (v. 41). God had prepared the way for the coming of the Saviour (vv. 16-23), he had sent the forerunner (vv. 24-25), yet the Jewish rulers rejected him (vv. 26-28). Paul urges those present not to duplicate their mistake. In their privileged position of knowing the background to all this, they have the responsibility of responding wisely and appropriately. Some did respond properly, finding salvation that day (vv. 42-43). The next Sabbath there was a massive turn out, but the leaders of the Jews, motivated by envy (as in Acts 5:17 and 17:5), contradict Paul. So Paul and Barnabas turn to the Gentiles.

The Jews have only themselves to blame for not receiving eternal life. By contrast, the Gentiles give the Word a glad reception.

In a typical summary (vv. 49-52) Luke reports:

+ the wider spread of the gospel;
+ opposition from the Jews;
+ the symbolic shaking dust off the feet (see Luke 9:5) showing the Jews' own responsibility for their hardness of heart;
+ fullness of joy and the Holy Spirit in the believers.

All along the way, Luke emphasises that this is God's work; it is his plan being unfolded. Luke's report of the Gentile response stresses God's part in all this: '...all who were appointed for eternal life believed' (13:48) and, 'God has granted even the Gentiles repentance unto life' (11:18). This response is not the product of human free will, rather it is the gifting of God.

(4) Mission in Iconium (Acts 14:1-7)

The ministry at Iconium is marked by bold proclamation confirmed by signs and wonders. And again, there is a divided response.

(5) Mission in Lystra and Derbe (Acts 14:8-20)

In Lystra and Derbe, Paul's first miracle of healing is performed. The parallel with Luke's account of the emergence of Jesus is striking. Luke recounts Paul's parallel experience to show that as Jesus the Saviour emerges, so his primary representative in the Gentile world has a similar experience. Paul is in accord with Jesus; Jesus continues his work through Paul.

Table 1: Similarities between Jesus' and Paul's Ministries

Luke		Acts	
4:1-13	Jesus confronts the Devil	13:4-12	Paul confronts Bar-Jesus, the child of the Devil
4:14-30	Jesus preaches in the synagogue and is rejected	13:13-43	Paul preaches in the synagogue to a divided response
4:38-44; 5:17-26	Jesus heals many, including a paralytic	14:8-10	Paul heals a paralytic

Paul's first healing miracle (14:8-10) is very similar to Peter's healing of the lame man in Acts 3. Both men were lame from birth and both were healed in the vicinity of a temple. The chapter 3 healing is at the temple in Jerusalem. Judaism could do nothing for the man, but Jesus heals him (3:6-8). The priests of Israel respond by opposing Peter and John and their message (4:1-3). The miracle in chapter 14 is through the apostle to the Gentiles and in Gentile territory. The nearby temple is that of Zeus, the supreme ruler of Mount Olympus and of the Pantheon of gods who resided there. The priests' response is to deify the missionaries, calling Barnabas Zeus and Paul, his messenger Hermes (14:11-13). Luke is showing a clear contrast in the response to the miracle between Jew and Gentile, while at the same time demonstrating that Paul's apostleship is of the same order as Peter's. Just as Jesus has worked through the one, so he works through the other. Both men, one to Gentiles, one to Jews, are apostles of the Lord Jesus Christ.

The response of Barnabas and Paul to this divination is clearly contrasted to Herod's response when the crowd attributes divinity to him (12:21-23). There follows a clear message to a pagan, agrarian audience. There is no reference to the Old Testament, no reference even to Jesus. This sermon is brief and makes no assumption about the audience's knowledge. Paul speaks in terms the people would understand. This is pre-evangelism. In his message, Paul makes the following points:

+ He insists on the humanness of the messenger.

+ God the creator of heaven and earth has shown kindness to you by giving rain, crops, food and joy.

+ People should therefore turn from these vanities (worship of men) to the living God.

+ God's attitude to humanity had been patient acceptance, but now all that has changed (see Acts 17:30).

This is exactly how Paul describes his message when he writes to the Thessalonians: 'For they themselves report concerning us the kind of reception we had among you, and how you turned to God from idols to serve the living and true God, and to wait for his Son from heaven, whom he raised from the dead, Jesus who delivers us from the wrath to come' (1 Thess. 1:9-10 ESV). But once more the Jews win the crowd round and Paul is stoned and left for dead.

(6) Return to Antioch (Acts 14:21-28)

The missionary team return through areas previously reached coming ultimately to Antioch where they report to their sending church 'all that God had done through them' (v. 27). Their return visit to Lystra, Iconium and Antioch was to strengthen and encourage the disciples (v. 22). How did they do this? By telling them realistically what was in store for them in their Christian experience: 'We must go through many hardships to enter the kingdom of God' (v. 22). Paul was able to say this with great integrity – he had just been stoned and left for dead.

We must not be unrealistically optimistic with new believers; unfulfilled, unreal expectations are always the key source of doubt. In training his disciples, Jesus placed considerable emphasis on the trouble that awaited them, so that when it happened they would neither be surprised nor overcome / overwhelmed with doubt (John 16:1, 4, 33). Both for the apostle Paul and for us, it is decreed that we bear the heavy weight of troubles to enter the Kingdom of God. Such warnings are given to 'strengthen and encourage them to remain true to the faith' (14:22).

From text to teaching
(1) Get the message clear
Big idea (theme)
Christian ministry involves the faithful, sensitive communication of the gospel (13:12, 38-39; 14:3, 7, 15, 21, 25). The messenger will be opposed (13:8, 45, 50; 14:2, 4-5, 19); will face many hardships (14:22); and must persevere knowing that God is co-testifier in the work. It is God who accredits the message (14:3, 8-10) and appoints those who will have eternal life through it (13:43, 48; 14:27).

Big question(s) (aim)
Preaching or teaching on this passage should answer the following questions:
+ What does Christian ministry involve?
+ What reception can we expect for the gospel?
+ Why persevere in ministry?

(2) Engage the hearer
Point of contact
In Australia it is a sign of affection to give a person a nickname. When I was training in college a fellow student who was bald was called 'Curly', and a redhead was called

'Carrots' or 'Bluey'. Sometimes, we just add a 'y' as in 'Cooky', 'Smithy', or 'Jonesy'. Often, the less attractive the nickname, the greater the affection underlying it. The marshal at our sons' school boasted that he knew the name of every boy in the seventeen hundred boy school. He had been a Sergeant Major in the British Army, so every boy, without exception, was named 'Sunshine'.

Luke tells us of two nicknames in Acts, one for Joseph the Levite (Acts 4:36) and the other for the followers of Jesus (Acts 11:26). But more seriously, he uses names to add stress or a note of irony to the narrative, to contrast characters or to point out their likeness.

So, what's in a name? A great deal for Luke our author!

Dominant picture
Newton's third law of motion states: 'For every action there is an equal and opposite reaction'. This law is illustrated when we step off a boat on to the shore – we move towards the shore and the boat moves away from the shore.

Spiritual laws are mostly consistent with physical laws. Here is an exception! The first Christian missionaries' law of motion: 'For every action there is always an opposite reaction. However, such a reaction is never the equal of the initial action.' That is, the gospel will always be opposed, but such opposition will never succeed. The gospel's spiritual power is supreme, making it unstoppable.

(3) Work on application
Necessary application(s)
We must persevere in ministry, knowing that despite opposition we are co-workers with God, and he will see his purposes fulfilled.

Refute impossible application(s)

While Paul is realistic about the opposition, the impossible application is that the forces of opposition will overwhelm us, requiring us to conform to them or cease persevering in faithful ministry. Because it is God's unstoppable gospel, we are on the winning side in the battle.

Possible application(s)

False expectations are the foundation of doubt. Do I have false expectations of response to my ministry? Do I fully embrace the inevitability of Paul's experience and words in Acts 14:22: 'We must go through many hardships to enter the kingdom of God.' In the gloom and pessimism often associated with ministry, do we recognise that our active co-worker is God himself? Is there a note of warning in my preaching (13:40-41)? The gospel must not be handled lightly, either by speaker or by listener.

Proclaiming the message
A preaching outline

Title: 'What's In A Name?'

Text: **Acts 13:4-14:28**

(1) **Cyprus** (13:4-12)
  + Bar-Jesus and the irony that he is a child of the Devil
  + Sergius Paulus and his likeness in stature to Paul

(2) **Pisidian Antioch** (13:13-52)
  + King Saul and his contrast with Saul
  + The divided response

(3) **Iconium, Lystra, Derbe** (14:1-20)
+ Healing of the lame man

(4) **A ministry pattern like Jesus** (Luke 4-5)

(5) **A ministry pattern like Peter** (Acts 3-4)

(6) **Return to home base** (14:21-28)
+ 'We must go through many hardships to enter the kingdom of God.' (14:22)
+ The Christian mission law of motion

Leading a Bible study
Title: **'What's In A Name?'**
Text: **Acts 13:4-14:28**

(1) Introduce the issues
Here is the first missionary journey of Barnabas and Saul. We can learn a great deal about what mission involves, what response can be expected, about God's active participation and the ultimate triumph of the work.

(2) Study the passage
Acts 13:4 – 14:28
i)   Why do you think Barnabas and Saul begin their ministry in the synagogue?
ii) Does Acts 13:9-10 represent an over-reaction to Elymas by Paul?
iii) Paul's sermon in the synagogue at Pisidian Antioch can be divided into two sections: verses 16-25 and 26-41. What is the main theme of each section?

iv)   Verses 30-36 focus on the resurrection of Jesus. According to these verses, what is the significance of these verses?

v)   According to verses 38-39, what does the resurrection guarantee (see Romans 4:25)?

vi)   Opposition is inevitable. How do Paul and Barnabas respond to it in 13:46-47, 51; 14:3-4, 6-7, 20-22?

vii) In what ways does Paul's sermon at Lystra (14:14-18) show his cross-cultural sensitivity?

viii) False expectations that go unfulfilled are always the cause of doubt. Why does Paul's realism in 14:22 evidence such loving concern? Do we strengthen and encourage others to persevere in this way?

ix)   What do Paul's and Barnabas' return to previously reached cities (14:21-22) and their appointment of elders in each church (14:23) tell us about their strategy?

x)   What is the emphasis of Paul's and Barnabas' report back to Antioch in 14:27?

(3) *Think it through*

Opposition to the gospel is inevitable. Patient, faithful perseverance must be the response of the gospel messenger.

(4) *Live it out*

i)   Do you have realistic expectations about what awaits you in the Christian life? To be a faithful witness will mean antagonism. Are you ready for it? Will you lovingly persevere in spite of it, knowing that God is faithful and will fulfil his purposes through you?

ii)   How can you encourage your fellow missionaries with these truths?

18

'THINGS WHICH GO WITHOUT SAYING'

(ACTS 15:1-16:5)

Listening to the text

This section has been called the centrepiece, the watershed and the turning point of the book of Acts. The meeting of the church at Jerusalem is framed by Paul's first and second missionary journeys. It is in the context of this work of mission that the church Council meets to consider the issue of the nature of the true gospel.

Things which go without saying need to be said! Since God is the author of truth and the gospel is his gospel, he will not bless a counterfeit gospel which is contrary to truth. Therefore, there is no more important issue than preserving the authenticity of the message which is to be preached.

(1) The problem (Acts 15:1-5)

According to verse 1, there were Jewish believers who were urging Gentiles who had become believers to be circumcised in order to be saved. In other words, to be Christians, the Gentiles must become Jews first. Christianity would then merely be a sect of Judaism. In Galatians 2:4-5 (esv), Paul shows what an important issue this is: '...because of false brothers secretly brought in – who slipped in to spy out our freedom that we have in Christ Jesus, so that they might bring us into slavery – to them we did not yield in submission even for a moment, so that the truth of the gospel might be preserved for you'.

I take it that the visit of Paul to Jerusalem described in Acts 9:26ff is the visit he refers to in Galatians 1:18. The visit with Barnabas mentioned in Acts 11:30 is the one referred to in Galatians 2:1. This visit to Jerusalem for the Council meeting is not mentioned in Galatians, as it is likely that Paul wrote the letter to the Galatians before the Jerusalem Council met, during the 'long time' spent in Antioch recorded in Acts 14:28. Galatians, therefore, knows nothing of the meeting of Acts 15, but provides important background for it.

The issue here is whether the gospel requires faith alone, in Christ alone, for salvation, or whether the work of Christ needs to be supplemented by circumcision and obedience to 'the law of Moses' (15:5). A survey of Galatians shows the danger of such an addition:

- ✦ 'I am astonished that you are so quickly deserting him who called you in the grace of Christ and are turning to a different gospel – not that there is another one, but there are some who trouble you and want to distort the gospel of Christ. But even if we or an angel from heaven should preach to you a gospel contrary to the one we preached to you, let him be accursed' (Gal. 1:6-8 esv).
- ✦ 'I do not nullify the grace of God, for if justification were through the law, then Christ died for no purpose' (Gal. 2:21 esv).

- ♦ 'O foolish Galatians! Who has bewitched you? It was before your eyes that Jesus Christ was publicly portrayed as crucified. Let me ask you only this: Did you receive the Spirit by works of the law or by hearing with faith? Are you so foolish? Having begun by the Spirit, are you now being perfected by the flesh?' (Gal. 3:1-3 ESV).
- ♦ '... for in Christ Jesus you are all sons of God, through faith' (Gal. 3:26 ESV).
- ♦ 'Look: I, Paul, say to you that if you accept circumcision, Christ will be of no advantage to you. I testify again to every man who accepts circumcision that he is obligated to keep the whole law' (Gal. 5:2-3 ESV).

Today our 'additions' may be good things, such as observance of the sacraments, following certain worship styles etc. But if any of these become compulsory conditions for salvation they become dangerously subversive, for they take our focus away from the sufficiency of the work of Christ alone to set us right with God.

(2) The debate (Acts 15:6-12)

Peter now makes his last appearance in Acts. His previous deliverance from prison in Acts 12 was to keep him safe for the vital testimony he would give to the Council. As the primary apostle to the Jews he is the lead speaker. He makes three points:

- i) He takes them back to Cornelius and points to God's activity among the Gentiles (vv. 7-8).
- ii) He shows that God is not prejudiced - the Gentile and Jewish experience of the gospel is the same (vv. 8-9).

iii) He makes clear the principle that salvation is by
grace, not law (v. 11).

Peter may have seen the law more positively before (see
Acts 10:14), but he now sees it as a heavy yoke which Israel
has never been able to bear (Luke 11:46). He says that laying
the yoke on the Gentiles is to 'test' God (v. 10) (this is the
same word used to describe Sapphira's lying in Acts 5:9).

Barnabas and Paul underline God's accreditation and
approval of their ministry to the Gentiles by telling of
the signs and wonders God did through them among the
Gentiles (v. 12).

(3) *The decision (Acts 15:13-21)*

James is the next to speak. This is James the brother of
Jesus, to whom Jesus especially appeared according to
1 Corinthians 15:7. James diplomatically refers to Peter
using his Hebrew name Simeon (v. 14 ESV), and yet quotes
from the Old Testament (Amos 9:11-12) in the Septuagint
(the Greek translation), probably because the church was
made up of a number of Greek speakers. He makes it clear
that:

+ The inclusion of Gentiles is something that God has
  promised to do. The restored kingdom of David will
  include the Gentiles (vv. 16-17).
+ The people of God will include Gentiles (v. 14).
  Therefore, no difficulty should be placed in the path of
  Gentiles turning to God in Christ.

(4) *The decision is circulated (Acts 15:22-35)*

These conclusions inform a letter to be sent to the Gentile
churches. This important letter is repeated in the text
three times: here in verse 20, then in 15:29 and again at

Jerusalem in 21:25. The letter asks Gentiles to refrain from habits which would make table fellowship with Jewish believers difficult, namely partaking of food offered to idols, eating meat improperly butchered and engaging in sexual immorality. This last one seems out of place in a list of activities best relinquished for the sake of fellowship. Surely there is nothing 'take it or leave it' about sexual immorality! The word for 'sexual immorality' is *'porneia'*, and could mean marriage within a relationship approved by Gentiles but not by Jews. Witherington identifies (pp. 460 ff) all of these activities as pagan temple activities. He concludes, therefore, that the letter is saying that these activities, so much a part of pagan experience, are no longer appropriate for the believer. In this case *porneia* would be sacred temple prostitution. Therefore, the Gentiles are to turn from idolatry and all pagan temple activity, including prostitution.

None of these instructions would be troubling or inconsistent with 'the grace of our Lord Jesus' (Acts 15:11). They would mean no surrender of gospel freedom, and would ensure the integrity of Gentile profession and fellowship in the community of believing Jews and Gentiles. The result (v. 30) is that the decision is circulated. The gospel's integrity is upheld, the ministry to the Gentiles is validated and the circumcision party is repudiated. Tension over these issues will still continue however, as is evident from Paul's ministry in Jerusalem in Acts 21-22.

(5) *Twin ironies (Acts 15:36-16:5)*
Two ironic events follow:

> **15:36-41:** In the midst of unity, there is the sharp disagreement of Barnabas and Paul. Paul saw John's departure during the first missionary journey (Acts 13:13)

as desertion (v. 38). Barnabas saw John in a better light, which Paul later recognises (2 Tim. 4:11). God's hand is seen in this, as two mission teams form to multiply the work. Barnabas and his cousin John go to Cyprus, while Paul is joined by Silas, a fellow Roman citizen with close links to the Jerusalem church, and an ideal companion for his next two missionary journeys.

16:1-5: In the midst of defending non-circumcision for Gentiles, Paul has Timothy circumcised so that he will be listened to and accepted by the Jews. Timothy was a Jew through his mother, yet was uncircumcised because his father was a Greek. Paul resists circumcision when it is imposed as an essential for salvation. But when there is no such demand, and it serves to facilitate the gospel's acceptance, Paul has Timothy circumcised - after all, it is a neutral surgical act. John Newton said of Paul, he was 'a reed in non-essentials, an iron pillar in essentials'. The next time you think of 'timid' Timothy, remember his ready submission in this matter at about the age of twenty!

From text to teaching
(1) Get the message clear
Big idea (theme)
God accepts all people alike, through the grace of the Lord Jesus Christ alone. Such grace requires no human contribution or supplement.

Big question(s) (aim)
Preaching or teaching on this passage should answer the following questions:

+ How can people be saved?
+ Does the work of Jesus need supplementing?
+ Does God treat all people the same?
+ Is God prejudiced?

(2) Engage the hearer
Point of contact
It goes without saying that we love our parents or our spouse or our children, but it ought not to go without saying! Things which go without saying need to be said.

It is taken for granted that to be saved, people need to hear the authentic gospel, but that must not be taken for granted and go without saying. Even in the midst of busy mission activity the gospel's content must never be taken for granted. The authentic gospel – salvation by grace alone through faith alone in Christ alone – must never be taken for granted. It must not go without saying. It is vital to get it right, and it must not be assumed to be right. Things which go without saying need to be said.

Dominant picture(s)
The imposition of God's law, or of any human requirement apart from faith alone in Christ alone for salvation, is a heavyweight yoke which is impossible to bear. Imposing such a weight is both hateful to people and is to oppose God, for he has purified the Gentiles, given them his Spirit and made them a people for himself, without any requirement to obey the law of Moses. What seems so spiritual – requiring obedience to God's law – is actually hateful to people and dishonouring to God.

The same word 'test' is used of Sapphira in Acts 5:9 and of others 'testing' Jesus in Luke 11:16, when they say he drives out demons by Beelzebub.

(3) Work on application
Necessary application(s)
The authentic gospel must not be sullied by 'additions' such as circumcision. The work of Christ alone is the all-sufficient basis for salvation. Our faith must not move from its focus on Christ. The gospel must be faithfully communicated without addition.

Refute impossible application(s)
As the apostles clearly refuted attempts to add to the gospel by fervent religious people inside the church, so we too must beware of this tendency and resist it whenever we come across it. Their message will be: 'The work of Jesus is not enough to give us peace with God. Salvation involves faith in the work of Jesus *plus* faith in our own good works.'

Salvation = Faith →Jesus alone
Salvation ≠ Faith →Jesus + any additive

The heritage of Acts 15 is that today, this minute, a sinner without circumcision, without baptism, without confirm-ation, may come to Jesus and by repentance and faith receive freely, undeservedly, immediately and forever the forgiveness of sin and the gift of the Holy Spirit. A warm reception into God's worldwide family should accompany this!

Possible application(s)
Are my standards of acceptance higher than God's? We must resist communicating cultural mores as gospel imperatives. A friend's church had their notice board graffitied. After the words 'You're welcome' was sprayed in giant letters, 'IF'. Is the welcome of our fellowship conditional?

Proclaiming the message
A preaching outline
Title: 'Things Which Go Without Saying'
Text: Acts 15:1 – 16:5

Why this is an important issue:
(1) **The problem** (Acts 15:1-5)
(2) **The debate** (Acts 15:6-12)
(3) **The decision** (Acts 15:13-21)
(4) **The decision is circulated** (Acts 15:22-35)
(5) **Twin ironies** (15:36-16:5):
   + Disunity (Acts 15:36-41)
   + Circumcision (Acts 16:1-5)

Leading a Bible study
Title: 'Things Which Go Without Saying'
Text: Acts 15:1-16:5

(1) Introduce the issues
The debate in these chapters centres on the content of the true gospel. Does the gospel need to be supplemented by human contribution, or is it about trusting in the work of Jesus alone for salvation? Is it faith alone in Christ alone, or faith alone in Christ plus my religious activities?

(2) Study the passage
Acts 15:1 – 16:5
i)   What were the Christian Pharisees urging the Gentile believers to do (15:1-5)? Why did they want the Gentiles so to act? Why is this such an important issue? (see Gal. 2:4-5).

ii)   Contrast the reception of the church delegates Paul and Barnabas in Phoenicia and Samaria (v. 3) with their reception in Jerusalem (vv. 4-5).

iii) What is Peter's argument (vv. 7-9)?

iv)   How does he interpret what the Pharisees are doing (v. 10)?

v)   What is the summary of his argument (v. 11)?

vi)   Why do Barnabas and Paul refer to signs and wonders (v. 12)?

vii) James refers to Peter's testimony and Scripture (Amos 9:11-12) as the basis of his judgment (vv. 19-21). This judgment is repeated in verses 23-29. What does it safeguard? Why should Gentiles abstain as in verse 20? Why is sexual immorality so unusual in this context? What guidance does this give to us as we seek to live together as Christians in the midst of disagreement (see Rom. 14:1-4)?

viii) Acts 15:36-41 takes us back to Acts 13:13. Why do Paul and Barnabas disagree? What is the result of their disagreement? How can you detect God's hand for good here?

ix)   Acts 16:1-5: Paul has resisted those who would impose circumcision. Now he has Timothy circumcised. What do these verses teach us about Paul? What do these verses show us about Timothy?

x)   Why is 16:5 such an appropriate conclusion to the section?

(3) *Think it through*

Salvation is by faith alone in Christ alone. The issue faced by the early church was the appropriateness of faith in Christ plus keeping aspects of the Old Testament law. Do you think the issue of 'Christ plus' is still an issue today? What might be the additives today?

(4) *Live it out*
Discuss the following:

i)   One of the first imperatives in the letter to the Romans is for the believers in Rome to see themselves as God sees them (Rom. 6:11). Too often we allow our relationship with God to be determined by our performance rather than its assured foundation, Christ's performance. Our relationship with God therefore becomes determined by Christ's work plus our work. We thus enter the kingdom by trust in Christ alone and continue in the kingdom by trust in Christ's work plus our works.

ii)   Be sure, God has destined us to walk in good works, but those works are not the foundation of our relationship with God. God is always satisfied with the work of Christ on our behalf - he sees us in him, so we are to see ourselves in him.

iii) Remember salvation does not come from Christ plus religious observance, Christ plus good works, Christ plus sacraments. All these are good things, but the foundation of an assured relationship is Christ alone. The problem with any supplement is that it implies that Christ's work is insufficient, and we can never be sure that we have completed any additive perfectly. Salvation is by faith alone in Christ alone.

19

'THE FIVE CITY TOUR'

(ACTS 16:6-18:22)

Listening to the text

Up until now the gospel has advanced in Gentile territory through the rural areas of Asia. People have been won over, but some could argue that they knew no better. Now the missionaries come to Europe (Macedonia), calling people to repent by recognising the Lordship of Jesus Christ. How will the gospel go?

Surely the gospel is boxing above its weight as it comes to the prosperous commercial centres of Philippi and Thessalonica, to the intellectual capital Athens, and to the capital of wickedness Corinth. How will the gospel go? Will it be unstoppable here as it has been before?

(1) The Call to Macedonia (Acts 16:6-10)

God is clearly directing the missionaries: they were kept by the Holy Spirit from entering Asia (v. 6); the Spirit of Jesus would not let them into Bithynia (v. 7). Maybe there were guards blocking the way? Whatever it was, the apostles understood it to be the clear direction of God.

Where were they to go? The answer comes in verse 9. Paul sees a vision of a man of Macedonia speaking and begging for help (v. 10). This was the call of God to Europe. From the outset, the team is working under the oversight of God.

(2) Philippi (Acts 16:11-40)

This is the city where Mark Antony avenged the assass-ination of Julius Caesar. In return, all its citizens were declared citizens of Rome. Significantly, Paul reminds them in Philippians 3:20 that 'our citizenship is in heaven'.

In the absence of a synagogue, the missionary team go to the river on the Sabbath, where they expect to find Jews and God-fearers. They find such a group and as a result of their speaking Lydia becomes the first European convert. She is a woman of means - she has a household (v. 15) and is a dealer in purple cloth. God is clearly active here, as 'the Lord opened her heart to respond' (v. 14). She and her believing household receive baptism, and extend an offer of hospitality which the missionaries cannot deny: 'And she persuaded us' (v. 15).

The next convert is a fortune-telling slave girl who, like the demon-possessed in the Gospels, shows real spiritual insight. 'These men are servants of the Most High God, who are telling you the way to be saved', she proclaims (v. 17). That's true, as were the demon's words in Luke 8:28: 'Jesus, Son of the Most High God'. But neither Jesus nor Paul sought that testimony from such a source, so Paul, like Jesus, casts out the demons. Earlier in Philippi, the Lord had opened Lydia's heart. Now Jesus Christ's name brings freedom to the Philippian slave-girl.

The third person Luke tells us about is the jailer. Paul and Silas, as a result of opposition, are stripped, beaten, severely flogged, tied up and placed in the inner cell of the prison. Surely now the gospel has come to a dead-end. But no, there is an earthquake, the manacles are loosened and all the prisoners stay in their cells (we don't know how Paul and Silas persuaded them to stay). The jailer is about to commit suicide but Paul shouts: 'We are all here' (v. 28).

The demonised girl had told the people: 'These men … are telling you the way to be saved' (v. 17). What is that way? We already know that it is by the grace of the Lord Jesus (Acts 15:11). The jailer asks: '…what must I do to be saved?' (v. 30). We don't know precisely what he meant by that, but Paul takes him at his word and gives him the complete answer: 'Believe in the Lord Jesus Christ and you will be saved' (v. 31). Faith alone in Christ alone. This calloused man, who had beaten and flogged them, now bathes the wounds which he had inflicted (v. 33), is baptized along with his believing family and 'set a meal before them' (v. 34). What a remarkable day for that household.

The church mentioned in verse 40 was very diverse: a woman of wealth with a household, a slave girl, a cruel jailer and his household, and some others. Jew and Greek, slave and free, male and female – all one in Christ Jesus (see Galatians 3:28).

Was it all plain sailing? No. The first record of Gentile opposition is verse 19 and it is motivated by commercial concern. The slave-girl's owners will lose income now the girl is released from her demons. But that's not the reason they give to the magistrate (vv. 20-21). Often the real reason for opposition is hidden by the presenting reason for opposition. Here the real reason is loss of income; the presenting reason is the encouragement of unlawful customs (v. 21). In Thessalonica the real reason is envy (17:5); the presenting reason is the defiance of Caesar's decree, 'another king, one called Jesus' (17:7).

The news comes to release Paul and Silas from prison, but it is always illegal to flog, and imprison a Roman citizen and to imprison a Roman citizen without trial. Paul and Silas insist on their rights and the magistrates are alarmed that they have done the wrong thing (v. 38). Luke records this incident of Paul and Silas claiming their Roman citizenship rights to help readers in a number of ways:

- If Theophilus was a leader in Rome, he could see that the Roman magistrates did do the right thing when they knew all the facts.
- The incident also shows that opposing Christians leads to regret on the part of the magistrates.
- And for the sake of the church in Philippi, and elsewhere, we are shown that the planters of the church were not criminals, but men of integrity.

Paul and Silas are asked to leave and do so in their own time after visiting and encouraging the church (v. 40). Paul had been stoned at Lystra and left for dead, now he had also been stripped, beaten and severely flogged. Don't gloss too quickly over the agonising pain involved.

(3) Thessalonica and Berea (Acts 17:1-15)

Thessalonica is the first seaport reached by the gospel. Seaports were places of prosperity and licentiousness.

Wherever men arrive from the sea there are red light districts to meet their needs.

For three weeks Paul explained, proved and reasoned in the synagogue that Jesus is the Christ and had to suffer and rise from the dead (vv. 3-4). Jewish opposition is driven by jealousy (v. 5), though the presenting reason from these loyal subjects of Caesar is that Paul and Silas defy Caesar's decree: '...saying that there is another king, one called Jesus' (v. 7). The Jews gather 'certain lewd fellows of the baser sort' (kjv, v. 6) to cause uproar in the city.

Paul and Silas then move to Berea where there is an examination of the Scriptures in the light of their teaching. The Jews from Thessalonica seemed to be particularly aggressive and pursue Paul and Silas even to Berea, a distance of 70 kilometres (40 miles).

(4) Athens (Acts 17:16-34)

The gospel now comes to Athens, the centre of intellectual and philosophical speculation in the ancient world. Paul is distressed for God's honour when he finds the city full of idols (v. 16). Practical Dr Luke shows his frustration at the 'airy fairy' Athenians who 'spent their time doing nothing but talking about and listening to the latest ideas' (v. 21). What particularly interested them was Paul's teaching on resurrection (v. 18). Greeks had no hope of an after-life.

Does Paul begins his address (v. 22): 'Men of Athens, I see that in every way you are pagan, empty-headed idolaters...'? No! He makes as his point of contact the altar to the Unknown God and seeks to reason with them:

+ You do not create a place for God to live – a temple; rather he has created a place for you to live (v. 24).

- God is not dependent on us; rather we are dependent on him, even for the next breath we are going to take (v. 25).
- God is not lost, we are! He has taken the first step towards us. He has created order so that we can reach out and find the one who orders everything (vv. 26-28).
- We are God's offspring, made in his image; he is not our offspring, made in our image (v. 29).

At every point the Athenians had minimised God and maximised themselves. Paul now comes to the bottom line (vv. 30-31). In the past God had overlooked the ignorance which leads to idolatry, but now he commands all to repent. We know that such repentance was the experience of those who believed in Thessalonica – they 'turned to God from idols, to serve the living and true God and to wait for his son from heaven' (1 Thess. 1:9-10).

Paul preaches wisdom to the Athenians, i.e., he shows his audience how they may harmonise with reality. The way of harmonisation is repentance. The reality with which to harmonise is (v. 31) the coming day that God has fixed when he will judge all people. Jesus is named in verse 18, but for some reason, though he is referred to, he is not actually named as the judge here. The proof that the day has been set is the resurrection of the judge from the dead. The resurrection of Jesus is the proof that the death of Jesus is not the end (as the Greeks maintained) but the end of the beginning. There is life beyond death and that life involves judgment before Jesus, whose own resurrection is proof of the future resurrection of all mankind. Reality is death and judgment. Proof of reality is the resurrection of Jesus. Harmony with reality is repentance before God. This is true wisdom.

The response is three-fold:

+ sneering (v. 32);
+ further enquiry (v. 32);
+ belief by Dionysius, Damaris and a number of others (v. 34).

(5) Corinth (Acts 18:1-22)

Corinth sat between two harbours; it was thus very prosperous and wicked. Will the gospel have effect here?

Again the Jews oppose (v. 13), but the Roman proconsul doesn't get involved (vv. 15-16). In light of the Jews' abrasiveness (v. 6), Paul shakes the dust off his feet as a sign of judgment on the Jews for their hard-heartedness. The missionaries leave the synagogue (vv. 7-8). Yet after such vigorous opposition the gospel still has its effect (v. 8).

Notice that in each city where there is opposition, the opposition is used by God to open up new areas of endeavour. They leave Philippi and come to Thessalonica and Berea, where they are driven out and come to Athens. They leave the synagogue in Corinth and come to the house of Titius Justus.

In the light of such consistent opposition, what keeps the missionaries going? Paul was not a loner; he had meaningful and supportive friendships (vv. 1-4). Paul was sustained by the timely arrival of Silas and Timothy and their good news about the church in Thessalonica (v. 5) (see 1 Thess. 3:6). Paul is given a promise by God (vv. 9-10) that he has many people in the city and that Paul will be perfectly safe until all destined to come to God through his ministry have come to God. God called Paul and Silas to this European ministry and God does not abandon them. Ministry will be a battle: they will be opposed, beaten, flogged, stoned, and left for dead, but there will be a Lydia, a nameless slave girl, a jailer, a Dionysius, a Damaris, a Jason, a Sosthenes and a number of others: '...no one is going to attack and harm you because I have many people in this city' (v. 10). God's message is unstoppable. He buries his messengers, but never his message.

Paul's ministry was persuasive (see Acts 17:4; 18:4). He says to the Corinthians: 'Since, then, we know what it is to fear the Lord, we try to persuade men' (2 Cor. 5:11). He keeps persuading to the end (Acts 28:23-24). The fact of God's sovereign control in the face of fierce opposition means that Paul never backs off in his ministry. Even before the court of Festus, King Agrippa says to Paul: 'Do you think that in such a short time you can persuade me to be a Christian?' (Acts 26:28). We are to persist in ministry, despite opposition, knowing that the measure of Europe's greatness, and the measure of any nation's greatness, is the measure in which she has obeyed the word to the jailer: 'Believe in the Lord Jesus Christ and you will be saved'.

From text to teaching
(1) Get the message clear
Big idea (theme)
The gospel powerfully brings change to the cities of Europe, but it is not without severe human opposition.

Big question(s) (aim)
Preaching or teaching on this passage should answer the following questions:

+ What keeps us going during opposition?
+ How did the gospel impact Europe's cities?
+ How powerful is the gospel?

(2) *Engage the hearer*
Point of contact
In his book *Preaching and Preachers*, Martyn Lloyd-Jones tells of speaking at the University Mission at Oxford in 1941. He preached at St Mary's Church to a congregation full of students. 'I preached to them as I would have preached anywhere else' (p. 129). At question-time afterwards, someone criticised the sermon saying: 'It could equally well have been delivered to a congregation of farm labourers or anyone else'. Lloyd-Jones responded: 'I regarded undergraduates and indeed graduates of Oxford University as being just common human clay and miserable sinners like everybody else, and held the view that their needs were precisely the same as those of the agricultural labourer or anyone else. I had preached as I had done quite deliberately.... There is no greater fallacy than to think that you need a gospel for special types of people.' The gospel for Europe's farmers is the same gospel as that for the philosophers in Athens or the merchants in Corinth.

Dominant picture
The city from God's lens – a swirling mass of humanity, prosperity, wickedness, idolatry – but God has many people there, who don't yet know they are his. The messenger must persevere in the work and as he or she does, the Lord opens hearts to respond.

(3) *Work on application*
Necessary application(s)
The gospel is powerful in every setting. Belief and opposition are the fruit of ministry; so the messenger must persevere in the task with confidence in God to do his work.

Refute impossible application(s)
Resistance to humble repentance by sophisticated intellectual types can tempt us to think: 'The gospel is not up to the task of converting men and women in this sophisticated, technologically advanced, prosperous, post-modern world. The gospel needs to be recast for twenty-first century sophisticates.' The gospel's reception in Europe reminds us that we must resist this temptation.

Possible application(s)
- ✦ Do I persist in the face of opposition to the gospel?
- ✦ When God sends workers into the harvest field they will not lack his support. Do I recognise my role as God's co-worker and support his workers and his work?

Proclaiming the message
A preaching outline
Title: 'The Five City Tour'
Text: **Acts 16:6-18:22**

(1) **The call to Europe** (16:6-10)

(2) **Philippi (16:11-40)**
- ✦   A city of Roman citizens
- ✦   Lydia (vv. 11-15)
- ✦   Slave girl (vv. 16-21)
- ✦   Jailer (vv. 22-39)
- ✦   The church (v. 40)
- ✦   Opposition (vv. 19-21)

(3) **Thessalonica (17:1-9)**
- ✦   First port city
- ✦   Opposition (vv. 5, 7)

(4) Berea (17:10-15)
- Nobility (vv. 11-12)
- Agitation (vv. 13-15)

(5) Athens (17:16-34)
- The philosophical capital
- Idolatry (vv. 16-23)
- Correction (vv. 24-29)
- Bottom line (vv. 30-31)
- Response (vv. 32-34)

(6) Corinth (18:1-22)
- The capital of wickedness
- Fellowship (vv. 1-5)
- Out of the synagogue (vv. 6-8)
- God's promise (vv. 9-11)
- Opposition (vv. 12-18)

(7) Return to the sending church (vv. 19-22)

Leading a Bible study
Title: 'The Five City Tour'
Text: Acts 16:6 -18:22

(1) Introduce the issues

We are at the point in Acts where the gospel comes to
Europe. Momentum is developing, with the way cleared
by the Jerusalem Council for Gentiles to join the people
of God without having to adopt Jewish customs. How will
the gospel cope in Europe's big cities of trade, prosperity,
philosophy and wickedness? The gospel is surely boxing
'above its weight'. How will it go?

(2) Study the passages
Acts 16:6-10
i)   How did the missionaries know that they were 'kept by the Holy Spirit', from preaching the Word in the province of Asia and from entering Bithynia' (vv. 6-7)?
ii) Why is this such a significant vision (v. 9)?

Acts 16:11-40 – Philippi
i)   What can you find out about Philippi?
ii) There are three converts mentioned:
  + How are they described?
  + How is their conversion described?
  + In what ways are they different?
  + What similarities are there in their experiences?
iii) What do you think the church at Philippi was like (v. 40)?

Acts 17:1-9 – Thessalonica
i)   What is unique about this city?
ii) Where did the missionaries meet, and how is their ministry described (vv. 2-4)?
iii) What motivated the opposition in 16:19 and 17:5?
iv) What reason did they give for their opposition (see 16:20-21 and 17:6-7)?

Acts 17:10-15 – Berea
i)   What is noteworthy about the people in this city?
ii) Where did the missionaries go, and how is their ministry received (vv. 10, 13)?
iii) Who is behind the opposition experienced by the missionaries, and how do the church and the mission team respond (vv. 13-15)?

Acts 17:16-34 – Athens

i)   What is unique about this city?

ii)   What distressed Paul and why did he find it so distress-
      ing? What particularly attracted the Athenians' interest
      (vv. 16-23)?

iii) How do verses 24-29 seek to correct the Athenians'
      thinking about God?

iv)   How does Paul show his sensitivity here as a comm-
      unicator? What can we learn from this about preaching
      today?

v)   What is the bottom line of Paul's address (vv. 30-31)?

Acts 18:1-22 – Corinth

i)   What can you find out about this city?

ii)   What challenges do you find here about working in a
      wicked environment?

iii) What special promise of God encouraged Paul?

iv)   Identify how on this second missionary journey each
      hindrance to the gospel and rejection of it opens up
      new opportunities for ministry.

v)   How does this encourage us as we face opposition to
      the gospel?

(3) *Think it through*

At every mission stop there is proclamation of the gospel,
a response of faith from some and vigorous opposition
from others. But God is sovereign and his purpose is not
thwarted. He uses the bad reception as much as the glad to
see his purposes fulfilled.

(4) Live it out

i)   'To be forewarned is to be forearmed.' We should not be surprised when opposition comes our way. So why are we taken aback by opposition to gospel endeavour?

ii)   How did the missionaries persevere in the face of adversity? What can we learn from them so that we also will persevere in the face of aggression?

20

'A MODEL MINISTRY'

(ACTS 18:23-20:38)

Listening to the text

Paul has established a familiar pattern of church planting:

+ he begins at the synagogue (19:8);
+ his ministry is focused on the kingdom of God and is intentionally persuasive (19:8);
+ Jewish obstinacy causes him to go elsewhere to teach the 'Word of the Lord' (19:9-10);
+ his ministry is accompanied by extraordinary miracles (19:11-12).

This brief report on the ministry at Ephesus follows Paul's initial contact there (18:19) and his commitment to return. It is sandwiched between two accounts of deficient men – the twelve followers of John the Baptist (19:1-7) and the seven sons of Sceva (19:13-20). Reference has been made to each earlier but the context here is important.

(1) *Twelve and seven*

The twelve are deficient because of ignorance of Jesus. Paul deals with their lack of experience of the Holy Spirit by telling them the gospel about Jesus (vv. 4-5). Like preachers after him, Paul does not preach the Spirit, but preaches about Jesus, for to know Jesus is to have his Spirit. All spiritual deficiency is met by knowing and trusting the Lord Jesus Christ.

The seven sons of Sceva (a Jewish chief priest of whom no extra-biblical record can be found) are deceitfully deficient. Like Simon the Sorcerer (Acts 8:9ff), they want to use the power of the Spirit and think that can be done apart from relationship with the Lord Jesus. This is very common today. People believe that they can access the privileges won by Jesus' work without any reference to Jesus himself.

The Devil is not fooled at this point; he is the father of fakers and Luke's account of his dealing with the seven is quite comical (v. 16). The Devil's superior power stands in contrast to their powerless superstitious spirituality. The resultant burning of the magic scrolls out of fear of God and the contrasting health of the Word of the Lord provide a further rich distinction – the magic scrolls in ashes, the Word spreading and growing (vv. 18-20).

(2) *Opposition*

The ubiquitous Jewish opposition (v. 9) is now accompanied by Gentile opposition, which does not seem to have been stirred up by the Jews. Like the only previous account of Gentile antagonism in Acts 16:19, the opposition from the silversmiths at Ephesus is commercially driven. Paul's insistence 'that man-made gods are no gods at all' (v. 26) is bad news for the sale of the silver shrines of Artemis.

However, in this case the commercial concerns are mixed with theological issues. Demetrius is concerned that the temple of Artemis, one of the seven wonders of the ancient world, will be discredited by non-attendance and the goddess robbed of her divine majesty (v. 27).

The silversmiths will also lose their good name, for they will be seen to be making counterfeit (fake) gods that are no gods at all. The irony is that, of all people, it would be hardest for the silversmiths themselves to believe that they were making gods with their own hands. Here is something new – the gospel is being opposed by Gentiles with their own strongly held religious convictions. Even though they are men of conviction, as of course were the Jews, they are also an example of deficiency, for without knowledge of Christ they are in the dark regarding God – no matter how sincere they are in their devotion to other gods.

The resultant outcry and the crowd that gathered in the theatre, which was thought to hold about twenty-four thousand people, lead Luke to record two interesting events. First, Alexander (v. 33) is pushed forward by the Jews to speak. He was either going to defend Paul or add reasons for opposing him, but he doesn't get the chance to make a defence. The Gentiles, realising he is a Jew and no friend of their goddess, howl him down. Then the city clerk (v. 35), who was the spokesman for the city council which met three times a month, successfully calms everyone down by reminding them of the appropriate legal channels for action against Paul.

(3) Return journey

The missionaries then sweep through Macedonia, retracing their steps on a journey of encouragement (20:2). They come to Troas where Paul had the earlier vision and call from the man of Macedonia. Paul speaks at a meeting until midnight (v. 7), during which Eutychus not only falls asleep, but falls out of the third storey window 'and was picked up dead' (v. 9). Paul goes down, envelopes the young man, who then comes back to life (v. 10). Thus Paul is shown to be like the Lord Jesus who raised the widow's son (Luke 7:11-17) and the twelve year old girl (Luke 8:49-56), and like Peter who raised Tabitha (Acts 9:39-42). Paul is in the same line of life-giving messengers of God, a line which included Elijah and Elisha.

Luke emphasises the breaking of bread at the meeting in Troas. He mentions it in verse 7: '...we came together to break bread', and in verse 11: '...he went upstairs again and broke bread'. Is this emphasis intended to take us back to the night Jesus broke bread with his disciples? That night included the upper room discourse, in which Jesus spoke intimately to the disciples the night before he was crucified. So also Paul breaks bread and then moves on to Miletus to have his last meeting with the Ephesian elders. What lay ahead for Jesus was his passion, what lay ahead for Paul was his arrest and many court cases, but before all that Luke includes Paul's 'upper room discourse'.

(4) Upper room discourse

These would be Paul's last words to them; the Ephesian elders would never see him face to face again (20:36-38). This is the only speech in Acts given to an exclusively Christian audience. He reminds the elders of what they already know – the main features of his two year ministry with them at Ephesus. The reason that he reviews and rehearses his ministry amongst them was so that they could duplicate such a ministry after he was gone. His ministry in Ephesus was the model for the elders, as it is the model for all ministry which claims to be apostolic today. He refers specifically to his model: 'You know how I lived...' (v. 18); '...Remember that for three years I never stopped warning each of you night and day with tears' (v. 31); 'You yourselves know that these hands of mine have supplied my own needs and the needs of my companions. In everything I did, I showed you…' (vv. 34-35).

From Paul's review we note that apostolic ministry revolves around the ministry of the Word of God. Paul uses four words in Greek, translated by six English words, to describe his ministry: preach, proclaim (vv. 20, 27); teach (v. 20); declare, testify (vv. 21, 24); preaching (v. 25). His content is 'anything helpful', 'the gospel of God's grace', 'the kingdom' and 'the whole will of God'. All of this has as its purpose the encouragement that 'they must turn to God in repentance and have faith in our Lord Jesus' (v. 21). Repentance and faith is the only way to link with Jesus who is God's cure for our spiritual deficiency.

In these days of little contact with one another (even though we live in such densely populated areas), Paul's description of his ministry in verse 20, 'publicly and from house to house', is a special challenge. Paul was not just a public figure, but a face-to-face, caring, involved, incarnational, visiting pastor. Paul ministered personally with tears (vv. 19, 31) and so we shouldn't be surprised at their tears as he leaves (v. 37).

(5) Paul's focus
Paul's review of his ministry in Acts 20 omits any reference to the extraordinary miracles which God did through him

in Acts 19. Those who believe the way ahead in ministry today is via a signs and wonders crusade or an 'Acts-led recovery', rather than 'epistle-led renewal', ought to note that Paul's rehearsal in Acts 20 omits any reference to the 'extraordinary miracles'. This is an aspect of his ministry which is not necessarily to be duplicated in the ministry of the elders. The gospel they preach has been accredited by extraordinary miracles; God may, but need not, keep on adding his accreditation.

In verses 26-28 Paul paints two pictures. First, he uses the language of the watchman in verse 26. He has sounded the warning; therefore he is innocent of the blood of those who fail to heed it. In verse 28, the compound verb, 'keep watch', indicates a careful guarding – in this case, 'of yourselves'. The first duty of the watchman/shepherd is self-watch, for without spiritual health he or she is no help to others. We must guard ourselves if we are to guard others. Spurgeon said: 'We shall be likely to accomplish most when we are in the best spiritual condition' (*Lectures to my Students*, chapter 1, p. 7). According to Augustine, such self-watch consisted of 'praying, reading the word and weeping' (*Augustine Epistle*, 21:4).

This leads to the second picture: the shepherd and flock (v. 28). Paul recognises that the church is God's, has been redeemed with the blood of Christ, and that God's Spirit has appointed him as shepherd. Thus he is accountable for the task of carefully watching over that which is God's. He must never stop warning (v. 31), for ravenous wolves from both outside and inside the flock will attack without mercy, seeking to lead sheep away to follow them (vv. 29-30).

Remember, this is Paul's upper room discourse, his last words to the elders. They are words which come with some weight – the elders are to be diligent overseers. The ultimate confidence of any shepherd is in God and the Word of his grace (v. 32), for ultimately the flock is his and is under his protection. It is his grace which will sustain them and in due time bring them home.

> *'tis grace has brought me safe thus far,*
> *And grace will lead me home.'*

We live in a day both of trivialisation of weighty issues and exaltation of the trivial. We must never allow the ministry of the shepherd to be trivialised. To introduce another picture: we pastors are doctors of souls, concerned with the eternal condition of our people. We must be vigilant physicians; we must examine, warn, teach, encourage and exhort each one night and day with tears. This is the model of apostolic shepherding ministry: the Word, plus personal integrity and spirituality, plus the watchman's sense of accountability, plus sensitive application to each person in our care.

(6) The church in Ephesus – a warning

In the early sixties, Paul writes to believers in Ephesus and tells them of his pastoral prayer for them (Eph. 1:18-23; 3:14-21). He prays primarily for knowledge of God, of his love and power and for their hope. He prays for a growing knowledge of the riches they have in Christ.

Some twenty or thirty years later, the Lord Jesus writes to the church in Ephesus through the apostle John (Rev. 2:1-7). He commends their hard work, orthodoxy and patient suffering, but says, 'Yet I hold this against you: You have forsaken your first love' (v. 4). Without love for Christ, hard work becomes duty, orthodoxy becomes bigotry and patient suffering becomes empty fortitude.

Today the city of Ephesus lies in ruins, surrounded by minarets and mullahs. It is evidence of the fulfilment of Christ's threat to the Ephesian church to remove its lamp-stand from its place (Rev. 2:5). Single-minded devoted shepherds are needed to prevent the degrading slide of 'first generation' godly into 'second generation' knowledgeable, and finally, 'third generation' worldly.

From text to teaching

(1) Get the message clear
Big idea (theme)
Shepherding God's people consists of persistence, while facing opposition in the task of preaching, teaching, pro-claiming, declaring, testifying publicly and privately to the necessity of turning to God in repentance and having faith in the Lord Jesus.

Big question(s) (aim)
Preaching or teaching on this passage should answer the following questions:

+ What is the content of true ministry?
+ How should we shepherd God's people?

(2) Engage the hearer
Point of contact
I once interrupted a game my young children were playing. It was called 'church'. Our eldest daughter was playing me, the pastor. She was calling for someone to move a motion, for another to second it, and then for them all to pass the

motion, 'All in favour say, "Aye"'. Our children pick up models very easily – much to our embarrassment!

In every area deficient models abound – in the sporting field, in parenting, in business, in church leadership. What then does a model Christian ministry look like?

Dominant picture(s)
Shepherding is the recurrent image Paul uses to describe the role of elders in the church. 'The flock' are those bought with the blood of Christ who live under the watchful care of the Holy Spirit. The shepherd is the appointed, ever watchful overseer, sharing the Word of God's grace, warning night and day with tears. A constant threat comes from wolves who are savage and unremitting, seeking to draw away whoever they can.

(3) Work on application
Necessary application(s)
Are we being faithful shepherds of God's people, recognising our accountability to God who appointed us to this task and who bought the flock with his own blood? If we are not in the role of pastor or other Christian leader, are we actively supportive of such shepherding?

Refute impossible application(s)
The model of ministry Paul provides challenges the individualism so prevalent in Western societies. In the light of his example there is no room to say that the people of God are on their own.

God's provision of shepherds for his people shows that he is not a disinterested onlooker, watching the affairs of his church from a distance. He is concerned for the state of the church, ravaged as it is by aggressive opposition from both inside and out. No, God redeems the church, appoints its overseers and sustains it by the Word of his grace.

Possible application(s)
Are we sensitive to the warnings of Scripture and on our guard against those who will not spare the flock?

What sort of a model ministry and lifestyle do I provide? In what ways does the apostolic model challenge:

+ my motives,
+ my character,
+ my strategy,
+ my lifestyle?

Proclaiming the message
A *preaching outline*
Title: '**A Model Ministry**'
Text: **Acts 18:23-20:38**

(1) **The gospel comes to Ephesus** (19:8-12)
+ boldly, persuasively
+ the Kingdom of God
+ the Word of the Lord
+ extraordinary miracles

(2) **Twelve disciples of John** (19:1-7)

(3) **Seven sons of Sceva** (19:13-20)

(4) **Opposition** (**19:23-41**)
+ obstinate Jews (19:9)
+ financially-vulnerable businessmen (19:24-25)
+ pagan worshippers (19:26-27)

(5) Resurrection (20:7-12)
  * Peter (Acts 9:36-43)
  * Jesus (Luke 7:11-17; 8:49-56)

(6) Breaking of bread (20:7, 11)

(7) The upper room review (20:17-38)
  * Word based (vv. 20, 21, 24, 25, 27)
  * tears (vv. 19, 31)
  * night and day (v. 31)
  * publicly and privately (v. 20)
  * accountable to God (vv. 26, 28)
  * warning, danger (vv. 29, 30, 31)
  * a model lifestyle (vv. 33-35)

Leading a Bible study
Title: **'A Model Ministry'**
Text: **Acts 18:23-20:38**

(1) Introduce the issues
Of all the ministries in Acts, Luke reviews only that at Ephesus. The Ephesian ministry is therefore the model of apostolic ministry. Knowing the authentic model helps us to identify the deficiencies in our ministries. Are we engaged in ministry that is consistent with the apostolic model? What more can we do to support such ministries?

(2) Study the passages
Acts 18:18-20:12
i)   How do Apollos (18:24-28) and the twelve disciples of John the Baptist (19:1-7) show us the need to clearly

understand and experience the gospel, if we are to teach others?

ii) The seven sons of Sceva, like Ananias and Sapphira before them, are playing a part (19:13-20). Who is not fooled? How are they exposed? What results follow?

iii) What are the characteristics of Paul's ministry in Ephesus (19:8-12)?

iv) Here is the second example of Gentile opposition to the gospel. Is what Demetrius says about Paul in 19:26 true? What are his concerns (19:24-27)?

v) Solidarity of God the Father, the Son and the disciple is taught elsewhere (see Matt. 10:40; Acts 9:4-5). How does the riot affect Paul and those in accord with him (Acts 19:28-41)?

vii) Paul sweeps through Macedonia. What is his strategy (20:1-6)?

viii) What is the significance of the resurrection of Eutychus (20:7-12 [see also Acts 9:36-43; Luke 7:11-17; 8:49-56])?

Acts 20:13-37

i) Paul details his ministry at Ephesus. What does he emphasise and what does he not mention? (20:17-27)

ii) Why is Paul spending time with the Ephesian elders in such a review?

iii) Since these men are shepherds of God's people, what must they do first and foremost? What must they recognise (v. 28)? What must they be wary of (vv. 29-31)?

iv) Why does Paul mention his tears in verses 19 and 31 and why does Luke mention their tears in verse 37?

v) What can you learn from these verses about the method and content of Christian ministry, and the character of the Christian minister?

vi) As Paul leaves, where is the confidence of these elders to reside (v. 32)?

(3) *Think it through*

We learn far more from models than we imagine. Paul's reflection on his ministry at Ephesus provides a model to be followed then and now. In what particular areas would ministers today be challenged by this apostolic model?

(4) *Live it out*

The Ephesian church was planted in AD 53-54. The letter to the Ephesians was written in AD 59-61. The letter to the church in Ephesus in Revelation 2:1-7 dates from about AD 90. What lessons can we learn from the final mention of this church in the book of Revelation? What are the factors which may lead you, or your church, to such a state as that described in Revelation 2:4? If it were happening, what should you do about it (Rev. 2:5)?

21

'O Jerusalem, Jerusalem'

(Acts 21:1-23:24)

Listening to the text

Paul has a conviction that he must go to Jerusalem, and after that, Rome (19:21). This conviction grows so that he is both compelled and warned by the Spirit (20:22-23) of the hardships awaiting him in Jerusalem. According to Luke 24:47 and Acts 1:8, the gospel must reach the ends of the earth; Rome was about as far west as you could go, apart from Spain, and that too was in Paul's sights (Rom. 15:24, 28).

There are seven distinct movements in the narrative, developing the theme of danger and rescue in the journey set before Paul:

(1)   Paul's trip to Jerusalem (21:1-16);

(2)   Paul's arrival and the meeting with James (21:17-26);

(3)   the Jerusalem riot and Paul's *first* rescue (21:27-40);

(4)   Paul's address to the crowd (22:1-21);

(5)   the Jerusalem riot and Paul's *second* rescue (22:22-29);

(6)   Paul's address to the Sanhedrin and his *third* rescue (22:30-23:11);

(7)   the plot to kill Paul and his *fourth* rescue (23:12-24).

(1) Paul's trip to Jerusalem (21:1-16)

Paul has been literally bound by the Spirit to go to Jerusalem (20:22). He is strongly convicted and goes even though the Holy Spirit warns / tells him about what awaits him (20:23). His friends also warn him: 'Through the Spirit they urged Paul not to go on to Jerusalem' (21:4), as does the prophet Agabus (21:10-11). His fellow travellers plead with him not to go (21:12). But he goes, insisting that he is ready to be bound and even die in Jerusalem, 'for the name of the Lord Jesus' (21:13). In words reminiscent of the garden of Gethsemane, his companions conclude: 'The Lord's will be done' (21:14). And just as it was for the Lord Jesus (Luke 18:31-33), Jerusalem will once more show itself to be a centre of aggressive opposition to the interests of the gospel.

The Lord's solemn repetition of Saul's name (Acts 9:4) is matched by the Lord's solemn repetition of the city's name, 'O Jerusalem, Jerusalem, you who kill the prophets … how often I have longed to gather your children together, as a hen gathers her chicks under her wings, but you were not willing' (Luke 13:34-35). Christ's pleadings are to no avail; the city and the Sanhedrin remain totally consistent. 'Was there ever a prophet your fathers did not persecute' (Acts 7:52)?

(2) Paul's arrival and the meeting with James (21:17-26)

Paul receives a warm welcome from Mnason and the brothers (Acts 21:16) before meeting James and the elders.

Thousands of Jews 'have believed', yet retain their 'zeal for the law'. The rumour has reached Jerusalem that Paul is encouraging the Jewish believers to ignore Moses' law, even telling them not to circumcise their children. In verse 25, James reminds Paul of the Jerusalem agreement (Acts 15). However, that agreement had to do with the Gentiles and the law, while this issue concerns Jewish believers and the law. Anticipating trouble, James urges Paul to join in the purification rites of four men, so everyone will know there is no truth to the rumour, and Paul will be seen as a respecter of the law.

As with all rumours in Acts, there is probably an element of truth here. There is no actual proof, but Paul's teaching about meat offered to idols (1 Cor. 8) and circumcision (Gal. 6:15) may well have been embraced by Jews as well as Gentiles in those cities. As in the case of the circumcision of Timothy, Paul's approach to the law is flexible where there is no gospel issue involved. His participation in purification rites could be seen as an unwise act of compromise – it certainly did him no good, as we shall see – but it can equally be seen as the outworking of a completely gospel-oriented approach. In 1 Corinthians 9:19-20 Paul states the principle: 'Though I am free and belong to no man, I make myself a slave to everyone … to the Jews I became like a Jew to win the Jews. To those under the law I became like one under the law…' In 1 Corinthians 10:32-33 he says: 'Do not cause anyone to stumble, whether Jews, Greeks or the church of God …' This is an act of expediency. However, whether it is a compromise by the author of Romans and Galatians is a question open to debate. Professor Blaiklock comments: 'He sought to love, to understand, to act in selfless humility.

The result, by that tragic irony which Heaven sometimes permits, was apparent disaster' (p. 172).

(3) *The Jerusalem riot and Paul's first rescue (21:27-40)*

Asian Jews (perhaps from Ephesus) incite the crowd with a familiar charge (see Acts 6:13). Nothing stirred the crowd in Jerusalem like the charge of speaking against the temple and the law, especially when coupled with the possibility that the temple's sanctity had been breached.   The people of Yahweh try to kill his messenger, and Paul has to be rescued by an unnamed commander of the Roman corps. Wisely, the Romans had placed their barracks near the temple and they are on hand to rescue Paul from his own people four times!

In the first rescue, the commander mistakes Paul for an Egyptian terrorist (v. 38). The contrast could not be starker. Egyptians of the first century were generally looked upon as unsophisticated and uneducated. Paul the well educated, Greek speaking, Hellenistic Jew thus stands on the barracks' steps to address the crowd.

(4) *Paul's address to the crowd (22:1-21)*

Notice how Paul stresses his Jewishness:

- He speaks in Aramaic to 'brothers and fathers'.
- He reminds his hearers that though he was born in Tarsus, he was educated in Jerusalem and was 'thoroughly trained in the law of our fathers' by Gamaliel.
- He openly declares that he had been a persecutor of Christians.
- He stresses the devout Jewishness of Ananias.

- He emphasises that he had been called by 'the God of our fathers' (v. 14) and that what happened to him was a theophany, in which he has seen 'the Righteous One'.

The Jewish crowd accept all this, which may indicate that a good number of them were already believers.

In Luke 23:49 we read of Jesus: 'But all those who knew him, including the women who had followed him from Galilee, stood at a distance, watching these things'. One notable feature of the passion of the Lord Jesus is that he went through it alone. Peter had denied him, and apart from the thief (Luke 23:42), he was surrounded by mockery and unbelief. Back in chapter 21 verse 20 we read of the elders response to Paul: 'You see, brother, how many thousands of Jews have believed...' (21:20). Yet where are they when the crowd erupts, beating Paul and trying to rid the earth of him? And where are James and the elders? Paul too faces the hostility quite alone. Later, at his first defence in Rome, Paul was to testify that he had been abandoned: "But the Lord stood at my side and gave me strength, so that through me the message might be fully proclaimed and all the Gentiles might hear it" (2 Tim. 4:17).

(5) The Jerusalem riot and Paul's second rescue (22:22-29)
Again, the crunch comes when Paul speaks of his calling to the nations; that God's purposes should include Gentiles (21:21). A riot breaks out and once more the commander rescues Paul only to commit his second mistake. He commands that Paul be flogged in order to extract from him the reason why the crowd is so upset. As in Philippi, so in Jerusalem, flogging a Roman citizen is illegal; and

Paul claims his rights of citizenship. It turns out that the commander had purchased his citizenship, whereas Paul, by contrast, had his by right of birth. A Roman citizen had to be treated by proper legal process and that meant, for Paul, a Jew, being placed under the jurisdiction of the Sanhedrin.

Once again, Roman leaders are seen in a positive light. If Theophilus was a leading figure in the Roman government, he would have been greatly encouraged that though mistakes had been made, the commander had acted with great integrity when these were pointed out.

In the attempt to kill him, Paul has been severely beaten. What a sight he must have been on the barracks' steps! He is rescued from the crowd which is venting its rage by throwing off their cloaks and hurling dust into the air. As he is stretched out to be flogged, we wonder, will he survive? Will God's plans be thwarted by such aggression? The tension mounts as Paul comes before the Sanhedrin.

(6) Paul's address to the Sanhedrin and his third rescue (22:30-23:11)

Like Jesus before him (John 18:22) Paul is struck on the face; and like Jesus, it is not apparent why his words should warrant such a response. Luke is drawing a further contrast between the Roman system which has treated Paul fairly, and the Jewish system which violates its own law and quickly degenerates into chaos.

Paul claims that he is opposed because he maintains the Pharisees' conviction about the resurrection. Once again the meeting erupts into chaos, and once again Paul is rescued by the Roman soldiers – this time he is in danger of being torn to pieces (v. 10). There was to be no answer from the

Sanhedrin to the commander's dilemma as to what to do with Paul.

Verse 11 is a wonderfully kind reassurance from God that no matter how dark things look Paul will testify in Rome. After all, the word of Ananias is yet to be fulfilled that Paul will carry Christ's name before the Gentile kings (Acts 9:15).

(7) The plot to kill Paul and his fourth rescue (23:12-24)

One wonders how long these forty men kept their oath 'not to eat anything until we have killed Paul' (v. 14). The trap is set, but Paul's nephew tells him about it, then proceeds to pass on the information to the commander, who is in a position to rescue Paul for the fourth time. He assembles an extraordinary detachment of four hundred and seventy men to take Paul, by night, to Governor Felix at Caesarea. There is no underestimating the Jewish opposition and Paul's case is treated with the utmost respect by the Roman authorities. The irony is that the Roman pagans become deliverers of God's apostle from the hands of God's ancient people.

It is profitable to look here at how God answers prayer. In Romans 15:31 Paul asks the believers in Rome to pray for his rescue from the unbelievers in Judea. We can't tell how he imagined that would take place; but it does take place. God answers their prayer and Paul is delivered four times by the representative of the Roman government.

The God of the Word is in control; Paul has testified in Jerusalem and now 'must also testify in Rome' (23:11). Paul is neither fearful nor uncertain. Rather, Paul's perseverance is fed by his trust in the sovereign purpose of God to see his Word fulfilled. It must happen: 'As you have testified about me in Jerusalem, so you must also testify in Rome'.

From text to teaching

(1) *Get the message clear*

Big idea (theme)

God directs the church's mission, he sustains the missionary and he sees that his purposes will be fulfilled. God himself is the guarantee of the fulfilment of his Word and the success of the mission.

Big question(s) (aim)

Preaching or teaching on this passage should answer the following questions:

* How much can God be trusted to keep his Word?
* Who directs and guarantees the success of the church's mission?
* In dark days, is there hope?

(2) *Engage the hearer*

Point of contact

William Goldman's book, *The Princess Bride*, has a character by the name of Inigo Montoya. In the film of the book, the part is played by Mandy Pantikin. Inigo seeks to revenge the death of his father at the hand of a six-fingered swordsman. He repeats: 'My name is Inigo Montoya, you killed my father, prepare to die'. Will he succeed? This question ratchets up the tension in this excellent story! And all seems lost when his father's murderer stabs him during a sword fight, but Inigo comes back and finally triumphs – though not without pain, suffering and great perseverance.

The plot of Acts has Paul coming to Jerusalem, but subject to much opposition. The tension of the story builds and the question raised – will Paul survive Jerusalem and finally make it to Rome, 'the ends of the earth'? This single question dominates the landscape of these chapters.

Dominant picture(s)
In this narrative, on four separate occasions, Paul is rescued from a hopeless situation. Each time the rescue comes from an unlikely quarter. This is the dominant, recurring picture.

(3) Work on application
Necessary application(s)
God can be trusted to exercise careful oversight over his church as it seeks to promote the gospel in the world.

Refute impossible application(s)
The deist has God the Creator retreating from the world he has made. God is a dispassionate, 'hands off' observer. But God's direct, verbal intervention in these chapters, as well as his superintending hand insuring the repeated rescue of his apostle, blows out of the water any notion that God stays at a disinterested distance, uninvolved in the daily outreach of his people on earth.

Possible application(s)
- Does my trust in God – the sovereign, involved, director of all things – show itself in prayerful dependence?
- Do I actively cultivate childlike dependence on him?
- Do I expect the unexpected in the way God will answer my prayer?
- No matter how bleak things seem, am I trusting him to fulfil his purposes?

Proclaiming the message
A preaching outline
Title: 'O Jerusalem, Jerusalem'
Text: **Acts 21:1-23:24**

(1) **Paul's trip to Jerusalem** (21:1-16)
(2) **Paul's arrival and the meeting with James** (21:17-26)
   + the accusation
   + the solution
(3) **The Jerusalem riot and Paul's first rescue** (21:26-40)
(4) **Paul's address to the crowd** (22:1-21)
(5) **The Jerusalem riot and Paul's second rescue** (22:22-29)
(6) **Paul's address to the Sanhedrin and his third rescue** (22:30-23:11)
(7) **The plot to kill Paul and his fourth rescue** (23:12-24)

Leading a Bible study
Title: 'O Jerusalem, Jerusalem'
Text: **Acts 21:1-23:24**

(1) Introduce the issues
Paul is compelled by God to testify in Jerusalem. All the pointers indicate that he will have a hard time. Will God sustain and protect him through these troublesome times, so that his Word is fulfilled?

(2) Study the passage
i)   Paul is compelled by the Spirit to go to Jerusalem (20:22), yet the believers in Tyre 'through the Spirit' plead with him not to go (21:4), as do Paul's friends in

Caesarea (21:12). The prophet Agabus also warns him (21:10-11). Why didn't Paul listen – after all, he had earlier (Acts 11:27-30)?

ii) What is the response of James and the elders to Paul's report (21:20)? What motivates him to ask Paul to join in the purification rites (21:20-25)? Why does James remind Paul of the Council's letter?

iii) Does 21:26 represent a compromise on Paul's part? What principles might have guided his response?

iv) The Asian Jews stir up the crowd at the temple. This charge (v. 28) has appeared before (see Matt. 26:60-61; Acts 6:13; 21:21). How valid were the charges?

v) The mob was aroused (21:30-36). Who rescues Paul and why is this so ironic?

vi) What does Paul's address to the crowd stress about himself and Ananias?

vii) What did the Jerusalem crowd seemingly accept from Paul's words about Jesus and his own experience?

viii) What was it that sent the crowd into a rage (22:22)? Why was this so upsetting for them?

ix) The commander rescues Paul a second time and for the second time makes a mistake. What are his two mistakes (21:38; 22:25)? What is his response to his mistakes? Why do you think Luke tells us about these mistakes?

x) Note the parallel experiences between the Lord Jesus and Paul at the Sanhedrin (Luke 22:66–23:5; John 18:22-24; Acts 23:1-5). How does Paul's treatment at the Sanhedrin compare with his treatment from the Romans?

xi) For the fourth time Paul is rescued by the same man (23:23). Why does Luke go into such detail here?

xii) Why would Acts 23:11 be such an encouragement for
      Paul?

(3) *Think it through*

Just as Jesus was compelled to go to Jerusalem
(Luke 18:31-33; Mark 10:32), so Paul is compelled to go.
Each has a different outcome and yet each outcome is clearly
under God's control. Consider: Paul is seized, dragged and
beaten by a wild crowd; threatened by severe rage; stripped
to be flogged by the Roman authorities; almost torn to
pieces by the Sanhedrin; and is the object of a binding oath
to be killed. Each time, when things look dark, he is rescued.
What does this tell us about the sovereign hand of God?

(4) *Live it out*

One thing is impossible for God: to act contrary to himself.
So it is impossible for the faithful God to be faithless. He
will keep his Word, no matter how bad things seem, because
he has promised and he will do it. Look at Romans 8:28-29.
How do these verses and this narrative in Acts encourage
your trust in God?

22

'TRIAL UPON TRIAL'

(ACTS 23:25-26:32)

Listening to the text

For the preacher this section seems to be heavy with legal detail. What is the relevance of all this for Sunday's congregation?

Three trials are listed:

* Paul before Felix (24:1-21);
* Paul before Festus (25:6-12);
* Paul before Agrippa and Festus (25:23-26:32).

This section is framed by declarations of Paul's innocence. Claudius Lysias: '... there was no charge against him that deserved death or imprisonment' (23:29); King Agrippa: 'This man could have been set free if he had not appealed to Caesar.' (26:32); Festus also adds, in his request to Agrippa: 'I found he had done nothing deserving of death' (25:25). Three trials, three affirmations of innocence. Why does Luke give us this detail?

(1) Why record three trials? To vindicate God's Word

Speaking directly to him, God told Paul that he would be safe in Corinth: '... because I have many people in this city' (18:10). We have that same direct address here: 'As you have testified about me in Jerusalem, so you must also testify in Rome' (23:11). Luke shows us that despite charges before tribunals, God brings Paul to Rome, in fulfilment of his Word.

(2) Why record three trials? To show Paul giving solemn witness

These trials also give Paul many opportunities to deliver his apologia in various contexts, most notably before the kings of the Gentiles (ch. 26), in fulfilment of Acts 9:15. 'I pray God that not only you but all who are listening to me today may become what I am, except for these chains' (26:29). Paul successfully defends himself on five different occasions:

+ before the crowd in Jerusalem (ch. 22);
+ before the Sanhedrin (ch. 23);
+ before Governor Felix (ch. 24);
+ before Governor Festus (ch. 25);
+ before King Agrippa and Governor Festus (ch. 26).

Paul speaks of his pastoral ministry at Ephesus involving testimony or solemn witness to the gospel of God's grace (20:24). According to 23:11, God sees Paul's role as bearing solemn witness in Jerusalem and in Rome. The term 'witness' is applicable not simply in a legal setting as here, but in a wider pastoral and evangelistic setting. It can be used to describe 'the task the Lord Jesus has given me – the task of testifying to the gospel of God's grace' (20:24). The word 'testimony' involves the speaker's personal involvement and guarantee of the truth of the Word being delivered.

Paul is testifying before five separate 'tribunals' on his way to Rome. His primary purpose does not seem to be to prove his innocence – though that also transpires – but to persuade his audience of the truth of his experience and to encourage them to investigate the issue of the resurrection for themselves (see Acts 24:21; 26:7-8, 23; 28:28-29).

(3) Why record three trials? To show that the resurrection empowers perseverance in testimony

One wonders how Paul keeps going, given all the trials and setbacks he faces. The key is the resurrection of Christ, to which he testifies so persistently in these chapters. Paul makes it clear elsewhere (to the Corinthians) that the resurrection of Christ keeps our preaching from being useless (1 Cor. 15:14), our faith from being futile (1 Cor. 15:17) and the believer from being pitied (1 Cor. 15:19). Because of the resurrection we know that there is life beyond this earthly existence and so whatever we do for the Lord is not in vain (1 Cor. 15:58). Paul urges his readers to stand firm and give themselves fully to Christ's work, because Christ's resurrection means that all of life now is a preparation for the life to come. Therefore the ministry of testifying, which makes people aware of that life to come, is never empty, vain or pointless. This is the conviction which gives Paul his persistent focus in every arena, whenever he speaks.

(4) Why record three trials? To explain the content of the charges against Paul

Some commentators, who accept that Theophilus was a Roman official, see this section as further evidence that

Acts is a legal brief in support of Paul's case as he comes to Rome. It provides a full record of Paul's 'suit' and would help the authorities in Rome make up their minds about him. It gives the content of the charges against Paul. Tertullus, after buttering up Felix (24:1-5), charges Paul with being:

- a trouble maker, stirring riots among Jews all over the world (24:5);
- a ring leader of the Nazarene sect (24:5). This sect was not a legally recognised religion and therefore Paul was alleged to be a dissident;
- someone who tried to desecrate the sanctity of the temple in Jerusalem (24:6).

All of which charges were supported by witnesses (v. 9). Again, many serious charges are mentioned when Paul comes before Festus (25:7). He, in his turn, reports to Agrippa that the indictments brought by the Jews against Paul were disputes about their own religion and about the death and resurrection of Jesus (25:18-19).

Paul's defence is built around his circumspect behaviour in Jerusalem and his thorough Jewish orthodoxy: 'I worship the God of our fathers as a follower of the Way, which they call a sect' (24:14). Paul raises the real issue at stake, his belief in the resurrection (24:21). Once again the real issue is concealed beneath the surface of the charges being made before the Romans. Paul declares his innocence again before Festus (25:8-10). And before Agrippa he asserts that his faith in the resurrection is the key issue (26:6-8). This assertion has ongoing relevance in our closed-minded and cynical age: 'Why should any of you consider it incredible that God raises the dead?' (26:8)

Another salient feature of the account is the importance the Jews seem to attach to Paul's case. In the first trial, Tertullus, a professional lawyer, leads the prosecution and even the High Priest, Ananias, attended (24:1). Over two years pass. Festus the new Governor visits Jerusalem, and the Jews 'urgently' request Paul's transfer. They have put a plot on hold to ambush and kill him on the way to Jerusalem (Acts 25:2-3). Paul takes himself out of their jurisdiction by his direct appeal to Caesar, the highest authority (25:11-12). Paul's persistence as a testifier is impressive, as is the persistence of the Jewish opposition. The gospel messenger can never expect an easy ride.

(5) Why record three trials? To show we've been here before

This section of Acts gives us something of a feeling of 'déjà vu'. How is it that a man, so often declared innocent, is kept in prison and transferred under guard to Rome as a prisoner? Paul was kept in prison because Felix thought a bribe was possible (24:26) and it may be that he also had a personal interest in the Christian faith (24:24-25). Politically, Felix wanted to please the Jews (24:27) and knew that Paul's imprisonment would do so. Paul's appeal to Caesar is brought about by the possibility that Festus, wanting to keep the Jews onside, would send Paul to Jerusalem to stand trial (25:9).

We have been here before. In Luke 23, the Roman Governor Pilate, in face of the charges by the Jews that Jesus claims to be a king contrary to Caesar, says, 'I find no basis for a charge against this man' (Luke 23:4). Jesus does not give any answer when he is accused before Herod (Luke 23:9). Then he stands before Pilate again, who says: 'I have examined him in your presence and have found no basis for your charges against him. Neither has Herod, for he sent him back to us...' (Luke 23:14-15). Three affirmations of innocence and yet Jesus is treated as though guilty. Pilate 'surrendered Jesus to their will' (Luke 23:25) and he is taken away and crucified.

God is in control of both these events. In one he brings about human redemption through the death of his Son: 'They did what your power and will had decided beforehand should happen' (Acts 4:28). In the other, he ensures that the message of redemption is brought to Rome, despite the best efforts of its opponents: '... so you must also testify in Rome' (Acts 23:11).

From text to teaching
(1) Get the message clear
Big idea (theme)
Paul the testifier (23:11) persistently focuses on the gospel despite equally persistent allegations and trials, designed to discredit both bearer and message. He is vindicated by the tribunal and sent to Rome under its guard, so that he can testify there also.

Big question(s) (aim)
Preaching or teaching on this passage should answer the following questions:

+ What does Christian testimony involve?
+ How does the testifier persist despite allegation and trial?
+ What can the testifier expect from the world?
+ What can the testifier expect from God?
+ How does God answer prayer (Rom. 15:32)?

(2) *Engage the hearer*
Point of Contact

We hate injustice; yet here is a case of not only double jeopardy, but triple jeopardy - one man on trial for the same crime three times. The Solicitor General for Scotland once said: 'But sir, truth will always bear an examination.' In response, Dr Johnson replied: 'Yes, sir, but it is painful to be forced to defend it. Consider, sir, how should you like, though conscious of your innocence, to be tried before a jury for a capital crime, once a week' (*Life of Samuel Johnson*, 2, Boswell p. 11).

Paul never seems to waver under the load of such unjust persistent examination. He keeps testifying in the face of great antagonism. How great is God to sustain such testimony under such difficulty!

Dominant picture(s)

We have strange contrasts here:

> Contrast 1: Prison is generally associated with guilt, yet Paul continues to be imprisoned despite a three-fold declaration of innocence.

> Contrast 2: Paul is the accused before the tribunal - but he doesn't act like the accused. His primary concern doesn't seem to be for his own safety or even his acquittal – there is no self pity about him. He is on a mission; he is to testify, and that is what he does in every arena, at every opportunity God opens up for him.

These are strange contrasts: an innocent man in jail, an accused man on the attack.

(3) Work on application
Necessary application(s)
Paul the testifier's courage, persistence and clear focus on the resurrection, trusting in God to fulfil his purposes – this is a model of testimony for believers in every age.

Refute impossible application(s)
Clearly the example of Paul shows that the following sentiments are nonsense:

+ That testimony and testifier can expect a universally warm reception.
+ That solidarity with Jesus will lead to prosperity in this world's sense.

Remember Christ's words: 'No servant is greater than his master. If they persecuted me, they will persecute you also' (John 15:20). As for him, so for Paul, and so for you.

Possible application(s)
We are to be testifiers, and our testimony is never unaccompanied (see John 15:26-27). Opposition will be persistent and must be met with persistent faithfulness. We must not be embittered by injustice, but trust in the just God and get on with ministry.

Show how these observations from Calvin work out in ministry contexts today:

+ 'The more brightly the light of doctrine shines, so as to press more closely on wicked men, they are driven to a greater pitch of madness' (Calvin on *Synoptic Gospels* II: 159).
+ 'No man is fit to preach the gospel, seeing the whole world is set against it, save only he which is armed to suffer' (Calvin on *Acts* I. 381).

Proclaiming the message
A preaching outline
Title: 'Trial Upon Trial'
Text: Acts 23:25-26:32

(1) **Paul is innocent** (23:29)
(2) **Trial before Felix** (24:1-21)
(3) **Trial before Festus** (25:6-12)
(4) **Trial before Agrippa and Festus** (25:23 - 26:32)
(5) **Paul is innocent** (26:32)
   • but treated as though guilty
   • like Jesus

Paul as God's testifier
You as God's testifier

Leading a Bible study
Title: 'Trial Upon Trial'
Text: Acts 23:25-26:32

(1) Introduce the issues
Paul asks the Christians at Rome to join him in his struggle by praying to God for him: '...so that by God's will I may come to you with joy and together with you be refreshed' (Rom. 15:32). God answers that prayer, but in a way that Paul could never have imagined. God is faithful, but surprises us in the way he brings about his purposes.

(2) Study the passage
i)   What charges were brought against Paul by the Jews (24:5-9)?

ii) How does Paul defend himself and what does he believe to be the real issue at stake (24:10-21)?

iii) Why do you think Felix sent for Paul and why was he fearful (24:24-26)?

iv) Paul asserts his threefold innocence (25:8). Why then do you think he appeals to Caesar (25:11)?

v) Why does Festus seek the advice of King Agrippa?

vi) How would you describe Paul's manner? The content of his defence? His purpose (26:1-29)?

vii) At what point does Festus interrupt Paul? Is this in keeping with his character portrayal so far? What does Festus find so unreasonable?

viii) Paul says he is speaking rational truth. He expects Agrippa to acknowledge this because of his belief in the prophets (see Acts 26:22-23). How do Moses and the prophets help (see Deut. 18:18-19; Isa. 9:6-7; 53:5, 10-12)?

ix) Why do you think the king terminated proceedings at this point (26:30)?

x) What motivated Paul here? How does 2 Cor-inthians 5:11, 14, 15 help us understand him?

xi) Why is it significant that there are so many clear parallels between the experience of Jesus (Luke 23) and that of Paul?

xii) If Paul's was a test case, why is his acquittal by the Roman courts so significant for all believers in the early church?

xiii) What do you learn here about God's ways of answering prayer? In what ways are you surprised by the way God is bringing Paul to Rome?

(3) *Think it through*

Paul's patient perseverance, his persistent focus on the weighty truths of the gospel (24:25), his courage and his persuasive manner are all part of the model he leaves us. God guides and helps him at every point. Paul's ultimate confidence is in the Word of God's promise (23:11). Paul's part is to be a persistent testifier.

(4) *Live it out*

i)   How are you challenged by Paul's example? God's Word of promise to you is that you will never testify alone (John 15:26-27).

ii)   How are you seeking to be God's active co-testifier?

iii) As a result of these studies in Acts, how can we encourage one another to be more outgoing to the world and engaging with the gospel?

23

'THROUGH MANY DANGERS, TOILS AND SNARES'

(ACTS 27:1-28:10)

Listening to the text

Having faced the man-made obstacles of court charges, opposition and riots, Paul now faces natural catastrophe. The gospel messenger proves unstoppable in the face of human opposition, but how will he cope when faced with natural catastrophe? In this section, Paul the prisoner once again becomes Paul the leader of men.

(1) Background and setting

Paul and his companions, Gaius and Aristarchus (19:29; 20:4), join a ship to Italy under the oversight of the centurion Julius, of the Imperial Regiment, agents of the Emperor. They are entrusted with great responsibilities such as the transportation of high profile prisoners. Julius, like the centurions before him (10:2; 22:26; 24:23), is a man of integrity. Luke, as an eyewitness, gives us a vivid, detailed account of the journey from Caesarea to Rome.

(2) *The danger*

It was after the fast – probably the Day of Atonement – in early October AD 59. It was autumn, and therefore late in the sailing season. This created some urgency, because the journey was perilous and the weather was closing in. Luke's repeated phrases emphasise the danger: 'the winds were against us' (27:4), 'slow headway', 'difficulty', 'the wind did not allow us' (v. 7), 'moved... with difficulty', 'much time had been lost', 'sailing had... become dangerous' (v. 9). Paul warns about the disaster and great loss awaiting them (v. 10) but his words are disregarded.

Julius listens to the pilot and owner of the ship; they want to get their cargo of grain safely to Rome before winter closes in (vv. 10-11). They also did not want to have to pay harbour fees anchoring over winter in a strange port. Inevitably, the 'north-easter' (v. 14) swept the ship along. The storm was a raging hurricane force, and even though all precautions had been taken and everyone on board helped (v. 16), eventually, 'we finally gave up all hope of being saved' (v. 20).

(3) *The security*

Paul now takes the lead because he has been visited by an angel with a three-fold message (v. 24): do not be afraid; you must come to Rome; God will keep the lives of those who sail with you. God sustains Paul as he has done before (18:10; 23:11). Confidently, Paul urges his fellow travellers to keep up their courage for he believes that God will do as he says. He is the God 'whose I am and whom I serve' (v. 23). Paul has never forgotten that first lesson from the Damascus Road (9:4): to persecute Christians is to persecute Christ. Therefore, to know Christ, to be his, is to be in solidarity with him, to belong to him and to be under his care.

Paul is hazy on the detail – he knows they will run aground (v. 26), that none will be lost, and that he will come to Rome. Luke goes on to recount how Paul's warning is fulfilled. Paul repeats his warning that only those who 'sail with you' and stay with the ship will be saved (v. 31). He encourages them that not one hair will be lost and urges them to take some food (v. 34). Luke tells us the exact number of those on board (v. 37). The ship was run aground (v. 41) and, although the soldiers wanted to kill the prisoners, they are countermanded by Julius. All reached shore safely (vv. 43-44).

(4) Paul versus Jonah

It is helpful to look at the respective experiences of Paul and Jonah. Jonah is not willing to go to his God-ordained destination; Paul is. Jonah is disobedient to the Word of God and escapes to sea; Paul is obedient to God and takes to sea. When a severe storm strikes each boat, Jonah knows that the only hope for his travelling companions is for them to throw him into the sea, even though they are reluctant to do so; Paul knows that the only hope for his companions is for them to stay on board with him, even though they are reluctant to do so and try to abandon ship. Ultimately, the compliance of Jonah's and Paul's fellow travellers ensures their safety in both cases.

(5) The unstoppable messenger

God's messenger is unstoppable; he will reach Rome. God has given his Word and no raging hurricane can upset his plan. Even the plan of the soldiers is thwarted by Julius. In his wish to spare Paul, he ensures the safety of Paul's fellow prisoners. Paul is God's and God providentially protects him and all those with him – two hundred and seventy-six in all – with every single hair from their heads intact! (v. 34).

John Newton began his career as a sailor on board his father's merchant ship in these same waters of the Mediterranean. On 10 May 1748, he captained a slave ship struck by a great storm off the coast of Africa. He cried to God for mercy and was delivered. He wrote of his experience, perhaps recalling Paul's experience in Acts 27:

> *'Through many dangers, toils and snares I have*
> > *already come,*
> *'tis grace has brought me safe thus far and grace will*
> > *lead me home.'*

Paul arrives on Malta where he and his companions are shown unusual kindness (28:2, 10). Even though he has emerged as the leader of the group, Paul is not above ordinary tasks such as collecting firewood (28:3). Paul is bitten by a viper, and as the snake hangs off his hand, it no doubt continues to pump venom into his veins. The people conclude that Paul must be a murderer to have survived such a great hurricane, only to be killed by a snake. This thinking – that a person gets what he or she deserves as an automatic formula – was operative among Job's comforters, among Jesus' disciples (John 9:2), and had clearly reached the people of Malta as well. When Paul suffers no ill-effects the general consensus quickly changes from murderer to god and, like the Lystrans in Acts 14:11, the people venerate Paul. When Jesus received the report from the seventy-two after their mission, he said: 'I have given you authority to trample on snakes and scorpions and to overcome all the power of the enemy; nothing will harm you' (Luke 10:19). Paul's solidarity with Jesus and his messengers is reinforced by the incident of the snakebite.

There is no evidence whatsoever that Paul accepted or encouraged the veneration of the Maltese. He does, however, go to the estate of Publius, where he heals his father and the rest of the sick on the island. Paul's active ministry on Malta is further evidence of his obligation 'both to Greeks and non-Greeks' (Rom. 1:14). This is a complete turn around. The narrative begins with Julius' oversight, bowing to the greater influence of the pilot and owner of the ship. By the end of the narrative, however, Paul is the dominant character and the others are not even mentioned.

(6) Structure
As can be seen from the proposed sermon outline, there is something of a chiastic structure to these events:

The prominence of Julius, the pilot and owner of the ship; the disregard for Paul's evidence

  The storm

      Paul's report of his vision of the angel of God and his statement of his faith in God

      Paul's advice regarding staying with the ship and food are heeded

  The ship is wrecked but all on board are safe

Paul is the prominent leader and overseer of the group on Malta; Julius and the others are disregarded.

The turning point and focus of such a structure seems to be Paul's vision. He sees that his safety is clearly in God's hands and has faith in God. He shows that all God has said will happen.

(7) *Five direct words*
On five occasions in Acts, Paul receives a direct word from God. The first two direct his missionary service:

+ Acts 9:4 - his conversion and calling on the Damascus Road;
+ Acts 16:9 - he receives the vision of the man from Macedonia.

On the last three occasions God speaks to him during times of great need:

+ Acts 18:10 - the Lord tells him to persevere in ministry in Corinth; that no one will harm him: '...because I have many people in this city';
+ Acts 23:11 - the Lord stood near Paul after the violent reaction of the Sanhedrin against him, to assure him that he must testify in Rome as he had already done in Jerusalem;
+ Acts 27:23-24 - the angel of God tells him he must come before Caesar in Rome, and that all who sail with him will be safe.

On these last three occasions each message is prefaced by the words: 'do not be afraid' (18:9); 'take courage' (23:11); 'do not be afraid' (27:24). These messages come at a time of great personal need. They are gracious, timely encouragements from God and each has the effect of promoting unusual perseverance in Paul.

F.F. Bruce comments: 'Paul strikes us as a man possessed of uncommon strength of will, not easily to be turned aside from the path which he believed it to be his duty to follow' (F.F. Bruce, *Paul Apostle of the Free Spirit*, p. 459). True though that observation may be, Paul needed encouragement, and in his darkest days God saw his need and graciously met it. What a privilege to be able to say with Paul: '... the God whose I am and whom I serve...' (27:23)

From text to teaching
(1) Get the message clear
Big idea (theme)
In the midst of crisis, God's Word sustains his messenger so that he stands out as the steadfast leader in times of stress. The key to his steadfastness is revealed in his confident assertion: 'I have faith in God that it will happen just as he told me' (27:25).

Big question(s) (aim)
Preaching or teaching on this passage should address the following questions:

+ How do we cope in chaos?
+ Where do we look in times of crisis?
+ Who can be trusted when life falls apart?
+ Can anything frustrate the purpose of God?

(2) Engage the hearer
Point of contact
First impressions might lead us to think of Paul as a super-hero. All super-heroes shine in the darkest of circumstances and Paul is no exception there. But Paul is the antitype of the super-hero. The super-hero draws on superior power,

superior ability, superior strength and superior knowledge, whereas Paul shines for no apparent reason – unless what he says about God is true. Paul's strength lies outside of himself. In fact, when he is at his weakest, then he is strongest!

God's Word is the foundation of Paul's confidence. God's Spirit is the source of Paul's boldness. God's Son is the single-minded love of Paul's life. For Paul, knowing Christ and making him known is what life is all about.

Paul is a model of child-like dependence. He is a model of a man highly esteemed by God – one who is humble and contrite and trembles at God's Word (Isa. 66:2). It is a picture rarely seen, a super-hero who is humbly dependant.

Dominant picture(s)

A man on a promise – serene through tumultuous seas, shipwreck, near drowning and a snake bite (see Luke 8:23-24). What sustains him? He has been beaten, stoned, left for dead, threatened with flogging. He is not a super-hero in any way. He is weak, poor, with some sort of affliction. He is a nothing, yet he says he has one thing: 'I have faith in God…' (Acts 27:25). And so he changes the course of human history. The narrative begins with Julius in charge and Paul a prisoner. It concludes with Paul in control and Julius out of the picture.

(3) Work on application
Necessary application(s)

- ◆ God rules even over the 'natural' catastrophes of life. He will see that none of them frustrate his purposes.
- ◆ The gospel's servant can trust entirely in God to fulfil his purpose: 'It must happen!'

Refute impossible application(s)
The detailed account of God's fulfilment of his purposes in
Paul's life, even through he is in the thick of adversity, provides
a lesson for all God's servants. However tempted we may be,
we cannot draw the despairing conclusion that 'life grinds
out a meaningless mix of life, death, good and bad. It has no
heart, mind or will. Luck rules.' Such a view must be refuted.

Possible application(s)
- How composed am I when either catastrophe or minor
  irritants come my way?
- Do I live as a person to whom a promise has been
  made?
- Are the promises of God the source of my composure?

Proclaiming the message
A preaching outline
Title: 'Through Many Dangers, Toils And Snares'
Text: Acts 27:1-28:10

(1) **The down side:**
- the weather (27:1-9)
- Paul disregarded (27:10-12)
- the storm (27:13-20)

(2) **The up side:**
- God's promise (27:21-26)
- Paul regarded (27:27-32)
- shipwreck – all saved (27:33-44)

(3) **The snake bite on Malta – the sick cured (28:1-10)**

Grace shall bring me home.

Leading a Bible study
Title: 'Through Many Dangers, Toils And Snares'
Text: **Acts 27:1-28:10**

(1) Introduce the issues
The gospel's progress is not stopped by human opposition. How will it cope when confronted by natural catastrophe?

(2) Study the passage
i)   Why do you think Luke gives such prominence to the weather conditions here (27:4, 7-9, 13-15, 20, 27)?

ii)   Acts 27:23-24 is another example of God's grace to Paul (see also 18:10 and 23:11). What effect did it have on Paul and his fellow travellers?

iii)   Why do you think Paul was disregarded in 27:10-12 and then listened to in 27:30-32?

iv)   Why are we told the number of people on board in 27:37?

v)   In what ways is the story of Paul's trip like Jonah's? What are the differences / contrasts?

vi)   What was the thinking behind the remarks of the Maltese in 28:4-6?

vii)   Why do you think healings have suddenly re-occurred when Paul arrives in Malta?

viii)   If Paul were to attend your Bible study, what reason would he give for maintaining his steadfastness during the storm and shipwreck?

ix)   In what ways can you be encouraged by his experience?

x)   How has God given you unexpected blessing in times of difficulty?

(3) *Think it through*

Paul's experience is one of being sustained through great catastrophe because he had been given a promise from God (27:23-24). For us, life is full of dangers, toils and snares. God's promise to us, as to Israel, is found in Psalm 121. So we, like Paul, have been given a sustaining promise.

(4) *Live it out*

Paul is composed under pressure. Stress, danger, catastrophe and opposition are all part and parcel of life. All people have to face the pressure of living in a fallen environment. Christians are not exempt from that, and in addition must face the extra suffering that comes from being opposed because of our stand for Christ. Are you composed as Paul was composed? (Read Ps. 121; Rom. 8:28-39 and John 10:27-30)

24

'Unhinderedly'

(Acts 28:11-31)

Listening to the text

(1) 'And so we came to Rome' (28:11-16)

We are now in the last stage of the journey to Rome
(28:11-16). The ship which brought Paul via Syracuse to
Puteoli, the sea port of Rome, sailed with the figurehead
of Castor and Pollux on its bow (v. 11). These were the
mythical twin sons of Zeus, thought to be protectors of
those who sail upon the seas. What an irony, that Paul, who
has been delivered by Yahweh from so much in his journey,
now arrives on the coast of Italy under the figurehead of
these two pagan deities!

Of course, Paul's encouragement does not come from
these two brothers, but from his brothers in the faith. At
Puteoli: '...there we found some brothers' (v. 14) and at
Rome: '...the brothers ... travelled ... to meet us' (v. 15). Paul
is heartened by members of his family, the family of God.
Luke makes a point of telling us that Paul thanked God for
this reception and was encouraged (v. 15). Remember that

Luke was one of Paul's travelling companions who saw all that he went through, yet he does not paint a picture of Paul as a hardened man, unaffected by the trials he had to face. No doubt by the time Paul reached Rome he was physically and emotionally exhausted. Not only had he faced severe hardship in his journey, he had also spent three months on Malta in active ministry. It is clear that Paul enjoyed the company of his fellow believers. When he wrote the prison epistles during his time in Rome he mentions those who are with him (see Phil. 1:1, Col. 1:1; Philem. 1:1). The support of the Philippian church, in particular, gave him great heart (see Phil. 4:10, 18). The very sight of the brothers boosted Paul's courage for whatever awaited him in his appeal to Caesar (Acts 28:15).

(2) *Paul meets the Jewish leaders (28:17-22)*

After three days of living by himself under guard, Paul meets the Jewish leaders (28:17-22). The Jewish ghetto at Rome is one of the oldest in the world, lying roughly half way between the Vatican and Colosseum. The visitor is surprised that in the middle of an Italian city, one suddenly comes upon an area dominated by synagogues, kosher butcheries and Hebrew signs. It was here, on the banks of the Tiber, that the apostle was under house arrest.

Paul makes it clear that he is entirely innocent of any charge that he had acted against the Jews or their customs. He is one of the Jews, so these are his 'brothers', 'our people', 'our ancestors'. He had appealed to Caesar because of ongoing Jewish censure, despite being declared innocent in every trial. Paul may have had every right to feel resentment, to have developed a 'them and us' attitude to his fellow Jews, but he never allows this to develop. Paul is at pains to emphasise that he has no axe to grind against 'my own people' and it is because of the 'hope of Israel' that he is in chains. He has no treasonable intention of laying any charges against his own people before Caesar.

The hope of Israel has been mentioned earlier, before the Sanhedrin (23:6), before Felix (24:15) and before Agrippa (26:6-8). Such hope relates to the resurrection of the dead and particularly to the resurrection of Jesus from the dead, designating him as God's Son (Rom. 1:4). Specifically, therefore, Paul is in chains because of his faith in Jesus the Messiah, his proclamation of the gospel of Jesus and, above all, his proclamation of Jesus' resurrection from the dead.

Although earlier charges that Christians were anti-temple and anti-law (6:13; 21:21) had probably reached Rome, the Jews reassure Paul that they have not received anything negative about him. Nevertheless, they inform Paul that 'people everywhere are talking against this sect' (v. 22), the term 'sect' having been used earlier in Tertullus' charges against Paul before Felix (24:5). It is not necessarily a pejorative term – it could just mean a party within Judaism, a self-chosen group. Yet apparently people 'everywhere' are speaking against it.

Stop for a moment and ask what it was that people found objectionable about the Christian faith. It has made a new community of compassion in the ancient world – a community of generosity which cares for the welfare of people. Surely the gospel makes people better - think of the eunuch, Lydia, the gaoler and his family, Dorcas, Cornelius, Barnabas, Peter, John, Paul – they are by any standard honourable, good people. What is it that people find so objectionable about this 'sect'? These days, why is it that people use the name of Christ as a swear word? It is all so irrational – exactly as Jesus said it would be! 'But this is to fulfil what is written in their Law: "They hated me without reason"' (John 15:25).

(3) Paul explaining, declaring and warning (28:23-28)

A meeting then takes place with a larger group of Jews (28:23-28). Even at this stage, Paul's explaining and declaring ministry is emphasised. His is a persuasive ministry and he continues to try to convince the Jews that Jesus is the Christ by taking them back to the Law and the Prophets. Paul is entirely consistent from beginning to end. At Corinth he explained that Jesus was the Christ (18:5), at Ephesus he declared the need for everyone to turn in repentance and put their faith in God (20:21) and in the gospel of God's grace (20:24). God promises that Paul will testify at Rome (23:11) and that is what he does (28:23). His persuasive ministry is mentioned in Pisidian Antioch (13:43), Thessalonica (17:4), Corinth (18:4), Ephesus (19:8, 26), before King Agrippa (26:28) and now here in Rome (28:24).

Paul's consistency is matched by the consistency of the Jews; as usual there is a divided response. Paul warns them about a calloused non-response to the gospel (28:26-27), declaring that their passing up the opportunity of salvation means that the Gentiles will have the opportunity to listen (28:28 [see also Rom. 11:7-12]).

(4) The triumphant conclusion (28:30-31)

Luke now concludes his account in 28:30-31. Paul's activity over the next two years is described as 'proclaiming the kingdom of God and teaching about the Lord Jesus Christ' (ESV). We are not told what happens beyond the next two years. Did Paul make an appeal to Caesar? Was he released?

Did he get to Spain? These are left as open questions. The gospel has reached Rome as God said it would (23:11).

The last two words of the text are 'bold' and 'unhinderedly', an excellent summary of the story of Acts. The gospel has proved to be unstoppable. It is unhindered in its journey and its messengers have been marked by their courageous boldness. It is fitting that such a dynamic narrative should conclude not with a noun or adjective but with an adverb, 'unhinderedly', modifying the participles 'proclaiming' and 'teaching'.

'Luke has reached the objective of his history by bringing Paul to Rome, where (albeit in custody) he enjoys complete liberty to preach the gospel, under the eyes of the imperial guard. The programme mapped out in 1:8 has been carried through' (F.F. Bruce, *Commentary on the Greek Text of Acts*, p. 543). 'But at the point where Luke laid down his pen, Paul – though in chains – and the gospel of God's kingly rule were irrepressibly surging ahead without let up or hindrance in spite of human opposition or nature's storms' (David Gooding, *True to the Faith*, p. 371).

From text to teaching
(1) Get the message clear
Big idea (theme)
The gospel's messenger reaches Rome and God's purpose is fulfilled. Boldness marks its proclamation; 'unhinderedly' describes its progress.

Big question(s) (aim)
Preaching or teaching on this passage should address the following questions:
+ How powerful is the gospel?
+ How does the gospel reach Rome?

+ What is God's ongoing purpose for the gospel?
+ What is the essence of apostolic ministry?

(2) *Engage the hearer*
Point of contact

Most of Sydney's old department stores no longer exist. One of the old stores was Anthony Hordern's, which took as its emblem a large spreading tree. The tree actually existed, and travellers on the Old Hume Highway between Sydney and Melbourne (now replaced by a freeway) could see the tree on top of the Razorback range of hills outside the town of Camden. The motto of the store, written underneath a picture of the spreading tree, was: 'While I live, I grow'. For Paul, life is Christ and death is gain (Phil. 1:21). As long as Paul lives he ministers; he doesn't stop even in the most extreme and exhausting of circumstances; he continues to preach, teach, exhort and persuade. While he lives, he seeks to promote the growth of the gospel. 'While I live, I grow'.

Dominant picture(s)

Acts ends with Paul 'safely' deposited in Rome, ironically arriving under pagan figureheads, superstitious twin demigods. But it is because of the superintendency of Yahweh, the only true God, that Paul has arrived safely as promised. And it is the encouragement of brothers of a different kind that helped sustain him during the ordeals of the journey. Empty symbols fade before the reality of the true God's character and activity.

(3) *Work on application*
Necessary application(s)

God superintends the activity of his gospel-bearer who perseveres in the most extreme circumstances. Therefore, we should persevere in ministry and God will bring his purpose to fruition. God will triumph, but not apart from human persistence, a capacity which He gives us.

Refute impossible application(s)
As with the account of Paul's journey to Rome, which shows God bringing Paul through many troubles, toils and snares, so his eventual arrival dispels any notion that coincidence rules or that chaos and luck triumph. God will bring His purposes to fulfilment.

Paul's ordeal also challenges the comfortable notion of guidance sometimes (erroneously) held in Christian circles, which states that when things go against you, you shouldn't persevere, as the difficulties could be signs from God telling you to give up. When it comes to discerning God's will, God's declared Word is always to take precedence over our reading of circumstances.

Possible application(s)
How much does steady, consistent persistence in ministry mark my life? How easily am I tempted to give up?

Proclaiming the message
A preaching outline
Title: 'Unhinderedly'
Text: Acts 28:11-31

(1) **And so we came to Rome** (28:11-16)
   + Castor and Pollux
   + The brothers

(2) **Paul meets the Jewish leaders** (28:17-22)
   + Paul one of them

(3) **Paul explaining, declaring and warning** (28:23-28)

(4) **The triumphant conclusion** (28:30-31)
  • Preaching and teaching
  • Boldly and without hindrance

Leading a Bible study
Title: 'Unhinderedly'
Text: **Acts 28:11-31**

(1) Introduce the issues
Paul arrives at Rome as God promised he would. This has been a journey to exhaust the strongest traveller! He is encouraged by the brothers' welcome. After three days he meets the Jewish leaders, then a large number of Jews. For the next two years he teaches and preaches to all who come to see him.

By God's grace, while Paul lives he ministers. Given his experience he shows remarkable endurance. Both he and the gospel are unhindered.

(2) Study the passage
i)   Castor and Pollux are twin brothers, the sons of Zeus, the protectors of shipping. Why is it so ironic that Paul should reach Italy on such a ship?
ii)   'Other brothers' are mentioned in 28:14-15. What did they do and what effect did they have on Paul?
iii) What does Paul say to the Jewish leaders about his own history (28:17-20)? What is the hope of Israel (28:20 [see also 1:6; 26:6-8])?
iv)   When larger numbers of Jews arrived, what did Paul try to do (28:23)?

v)   Where else in Acts do we read of such a response as in
      28:24-25?

vi)   Note the context of 28:26-27. How similar is it to
      the context in which Jesus quoted these verses (see
      Luke 8:10)?

vii) Verses 23-28 tell us what Paul did for one day. Verses
      30-31 tell us what Paul did for two years. What did he
      do and to whom?

viii) What do you think happened after these two years?

ix)   Why is verse 31 such an appropriate ending to Acts?

x)   What are the big lessons of Acts? In what ways has
      Acts been a tonic to you in the realm of the Spirit?

(3) *Think it through*

Paul is in his mid to late fifties. He has come through an
exhausting storm and shipwreck, has been washed up on
a beach, bitten by a viper and has walked from Puteoli to
Rome (140 miles, 220 kilometres). After three days, he
begins ministry in Rome – explaining, declaring (v. 23),
preaching and teaching (v. 31). He is a remarkable example
of perseverance, a man driven by God's promise and enabled
by God's Spirit.

(4) *Live it out*

God's gospel is unstoppable and its messenger, who still has
work to do, is unstoppable as well. How should these facts
affect the way you think about:

    ◆   your life?
    ◆   your ministry?
    ◆   mission?

Appendix
FURTHER RESOURCES FOR
TEACHING ACTS

F.F. Bruce, *Commentary on the Book of Acts*, 3rd ed. (Michigan, Eerdmans, 1990). Succinct and clear. Available on both the English and Greek text.

J.R.W. Stott, *The Message of Acts* (Leicester, IVP, 1990). Outstanding for its clarity.

W.H. Griffith Thomas, *Apostles: Outline Studies in Primitive Christianity* (Chicago Bible Institute Colportage Association). Excellent for structure.

G. Campbell Morgan, *The Acts of the Apostles*, (London, Pickering & Inglis, 1974). Like Matthew Henry's commentary in the 6 volume series, offers excellent and helpful insights into the text.

Matthew Henry's *Commentary*, Vol. 6 (Virginia, MacDonald Publishing Company). (See the article, 'Great Value of Matthew Henry's *Commentary*', reprinted from a leaflet by W.F. Bell in 'The Banner of Truth Magazine' 274:25-26).

Robert C. Tannehill, *The Narrative Unity of Luke-Acts: A Literary Interpretation* (Philadelphia, Fortress Press, 1990). Good for identifying the literary connections in the text.

Tyndale Press has two commentaries on Acts, one by Prof. E.M. Blaiklock (*Acts*, 1959) and the more recent one by I. Howard Marshall, (*Acts*, 1980). Both preacher friendly, noted for their succinctness.

Ben Witherington, *The Acts of the Apostles: A SocioRhetorical Commentary* (Michigan, Eerdmans, 1998). The largest, most exhaustive commentary.

Dennis E. Johnson, *The Message of Acts in the History of Redemption*, (New Jersey, P&R Publishing, 1997). More a book on themes and the biblical theology of Acts, he makes lots of connections to the Old Testament; stronger on fulfilment themes.

Dennis E. Johnson, *Let's Study Acts* (Edinburgh, Banner of Truth, 2003). A good lay-level commentary, excellent explanations and easy to follow.

Chris Green, *The Word of His Grace. A Guide to Teaching and Preaching from Acts* (Leicester, IVP, 2005). Writing in 'Evangelicals Now', Chris Kelly of Lansdowne Baptist Church, Bournemouth comments, '...explaining Acts to me better than any commentary that I had read'. Provides a good broad overview of Acts together with selected sermons from Acts. It's good to see some sermons getting into print!

F.F. Bruce, *Paul, Apostle of the Free Spirit*, (Exeter, Paternoster Press, 1977). All you need to know about Paul! Very helpful index with cross references to Acts.

J.O. Sanders, *Paul the Leader*, (Colorado, NavPress, 1984). Helpful material for the preacher on the life of Paul.

I put Gordon Keddie's commentary in the Welwyn Commentaries series, *You are my Witnesses* (Darlington, Evangelical Press, 1993) and David Gooding's commentary, *True to the Faith* (London, Hodder & Stoughton, 1990) on a par. I read them both and found they were heart-warming, rewarding, insightful and read like preached material. Both authors are courageous appliers of the Word.

F. Scott Spencer, *Journeying Through Acts: A Literary-Cultural Reading* (Massachusetts, Hendrickson Publishers, 2004). If I had to choose one commentary this would be it, giving us excellent insights into the text itself.

PT Media Resources

PT Resources, a ministry of The Proclamation Trust, provides a range of multimedia resources for preachers and Bible teachers.

Teach the Bible Series (Christian Focus & PT Resources)
The Teaching the Bible Series, published jointly with Christian Focus Publications, is written by preachers, for preachers, and is specifically geared to the purpose of God's Word – its proclamation as living truth. Books in the series aim to help the reader move beyond simply understanding a text to communicating and applying it.

Current titles include: *Teaching Numbers, Teaching Isaiah, Teaching Amos, Teaching Matthew, Teaching John, Teaching Acts, Teaching Romans, Teaching Ephesians, Teaching 1 and 2 Thessalonians, Teaching 1 Timothy, Teaching 2 Timothy, Teaching 1 Peter, Bible Delight, Burning Hearts, Hearing the Spirit, Spirit of Truth, Teaching the Christian Hope, The Ministry Medical* and *The Priority of Preaching.*

Practical Preacher series

PT Resources publish a number of books addressing practical issues for preachers. These include *The Priority of Preaching, Bible Delight, Hearing the Spirit* and *The Ministry Medical*.

Online resources

We publish a large number of audio resources online, all of which are free to download. These are searchable through our website by speaker, date, topic and Bible book. The resources include:

+ sermon series; examples of great preaching which not only demonstrate faithful principles but which will refresh and encourage the heart of the preacher
+ instructions; audio which helps the teacher or preacher understand, open up and teach individual books of the Bible by getting to grips with their central message and purpose
+ conference recordings; audio from all our conferences including the annual Evangelical Ministry Assembly. These talks discuss ministry and preaching issues.

An increasing number of resources are also available in video download form.

Online DVD

PT Resources have recently published online our collection of instructional videos by David Jackman. This material has been taught over the past 20 years on our PT Cornhill training course and around the world. It gives step by step instructions on handling each genre of biblical literature. There is also an online workbook. The videos are suitable for preachers and those teaching the Bible in a variety of different contexts. Access to all the videos is free of charge.

The Proclaimer

Visit the Proclaimer blog for regular updates on matters to do with preaching. This is a short, punchy blog refreshed daily which is written by preachers and for preachers. It can be accessed via the PT website or through www.theproclaimer.org.uk.

Christian Focus Publications

Our mission statement –

STAYING FAITHFUL
In dependence upon God we seek to impact the world through literature faithful to His infallible Word, the Bible. Our aim is to ensure that the Lord Jesus Christ is presented as the only hope to obtain forgiveness of sin, live a useful life and look forward to heaven with Him.

Our Books are published in four imprints:

CHRISTIAN
FOCUS

popular works including biographies, commentaries, basic doctrine and Christian living.

CHRISTIAN
HERITAGE

books representing some of the best material from the rich heritage of the church.

MENTOR

books written at a level suitable for Bible College and seminary students, pastors, and other serious readers. The imprint includes commentaries, doctrinal studies, examination of current issues and church history.

CF4•K

children's books for quality Bible teaching and for all age groups: Sunday school curriculum, puzzle and activity books; personal and family devotional titles, biographies and inspirational stories – because you are never too young to know Jesus!

Christian Focus Publications Ltd,
Geanies House, Fearn, Ross-shire,
IV20 1TW, Scotland, United Kingdom.
www.christianfocus.com